C000228167

# RORKE'S DRIFT
# 1879

# RORKE'S DRIFT
# 1879

## EDMUND YORKE

For Louise, Madeleine and Emily

First published 2012 by
Spellmount, an imprint of
The History Press
The Mill, Brimscombe Port
Stroud, Gloucestershire, GL5 2QG
www.thehistorypress.co.uk

© The History Press, 2012

The right of Edmund Yorke to be identified as the Author
of this work has been asserted in accordance with the
Copyrights, Designs and Patents Act 1988.

British Library Cataloguing in Publication Data.
A catalogue record for this book is available from the British Library.

ISBN 978 0 7524 6400 8

Typesetting and origination by The History Press
Printed in Malta
Manufacturing managed by Jellyfish Print Solutions Ltd

# CONTENTS

# ACKNOWLEDGEMENTS

I wish to express my gratitude to many individuals who contributed to this work. The librarians, curators and archivists of the universities of Oxford and Cambridge; the National Army Museum; the London Library; the National Archives, Kew; the Gloucestershire County Records Office; and the Royal Regiment of Wales Museum in Brecon have been particularly helpful. Andrew Orgill, Senior Librarian of RMA Sandhurst Library, and his assistants, Ken Franklin and John Pearce, have provided their usual sterling and often exceptional support. The commissioning editor Jo de Vries and her team at Spellmount have also provided invaluable support, advice and encouragement.

The works and advice of several leading authors and experts in the field, notably Professor John Laband, Mr Ian Knight, John Young, Ron Lock, Peter Quantrill, Lieutenant-Colonel Mike Snook and the late, much-lamented David Rattray, Donald Morris and Frank Emery, have, over the years, jointly provided great inspiration for this book. My most recent 2004 visit to the Rorke's Drift battlefield and attendance at the splendid 125th commemorative dinner held in Isandlwana Lodge, so charmingly hosted by Pat Stubbs, enabled me to renew many old acquaintances and make many new ones. Major Andrew Banks and John Young both provided excellent pictorial support from their extensive private collections to supplement my own field photographs. Mr F.W. Jackson has been a source of great advice and encouragement and the several meetings and dinners we have recently enjoyed together remain treasured memories. Above all, I must thank my great friend Colonel Ian Bennett (RASC retired). Our regular triennial lunches at RMA Sandhurst and joint excursions and research trips have been a wonderful source of intellectual advice and encouragement. Several of my colleagues at RMA Sandhurst have also been of great help, notably my current Head of Department, Dr Duncan Anderson, MA, Dr Gregory Fremont-Barnes, Professor Christopher Duffy, Dr Matthew Bennett and Mr Sean McKnight, MA, Director of Studies. Mention must also be made of the scores of officer cadets and commissioned officers who, over the past twenty-two years, have shared my great enthusiasm for this famous battle.

Above all I must express my deep love and appreciation for the long suffering support of my family, especially my dear wife Louise and daughters, Madeleine and Emily, the former for the long tedious hours of rapid word processing of reams of documents and indecipherable notes, and, the latter, for the many hours of neglect by their elusive Daddy.

# INTRODUCTION

I was left behind at a place called Rorke's Drift... four thousand of them paid us a visit. When I beheld this swarm I said to myself, 'All up now', but I was wrong and we all agreed to fight till only two were left and these were to shoot themselves... The general said we were a brave little garrison and this showed what a few men could do if they only had the pluck.

Gunner Howard to family, 25 March 1879,
from Emery, *Red Soldier*, pp.133–4

The dead Zulu lay in piles, in some places as high as the top of the parapet. Some (were) killed by bullets, and the wounds, at that short range, were ghastly but very many were killed by the bayonet. The attack most have been very well pushed home and both sides deserve the credit.

Cmdt Hamilton-Browne, *Lost Legionary*

Fought on the night of 22/23 January 1879 and immortalised in the film epic *Zulu*, Rorke's Drift represented one of the most glorious, if subsequently controversial, episodes in British military history. For around twelve desperate hours, outnumbered by over 25:1, barely 140 British and colonial soldiers, based at the remote mission station of Rorke's Drift, Natal, South Africa, were locked in a furious life-or-death struggle with up to 4,000 seasoned Zulu warriors of the hitherto victorious Zulu Army – the most powerful indigenous African army of the day. The sheer horror, brutality and intensity of the battle in which no prisoners were taken, matched that of other much larger scale historical sieges such as the Alamo. Only hours earlier, in the shadow of the ominous Sphinx-like Isandlwana Crag, other elements of the same Zulu contingent had virtually annihilated a 1,700-strong British colonial force – one of the greatest defeats of Queen Victoria's reign. In the wake of this terrible massacre, the survival of the British Empire in South Africa momentarily rested with the tiny garrison of Rorke's Drift.

The main aim of this short introductory book is, by using revised material drawn mainly from my extensive published literature on the Anglo-Zulu War, my own fieldwork studies of the Rorke's Drift battlefield in 1989 and 2004, as well as that of several selected leading contemporary experts, present, for non-specialists and general history enthusiasts, a clear, hopefully balanced and concise analytical narrative of this epic encounter. The opinions expressed in this book are my own and do not reflect those of either the Ministry of Defence or the Royal Military Academy Sandhurst.

# HISTORICAL BACKGROUND

## Racial Friction

The long-term origins of the Anglo-Zulu War can be traced back to the arrival of the first European settler communities on the South African coast in the mid-nineteenth century. After the Dutch had established a major settlement in Cape Town in 1652, they were superseded, after a limited penetration of the African hinterland, by the British who promptly occupied this crucial strategic area during the Napoleonic Wars. In 1814 the Cape was formally annexed by Britain.

British political and economic pressures, notably the imposition of regularised taxation and the abolition of slavery, encouraged many of the fiercely independent and largely agrarian-based and slave-owning original Dutch settlers or 'Boers' to trek deep into the interior. By the end of the 1830s hundreds of Boer farmers were leaving to escape British rule and, by the 1850s, they had set up two independent republics traversing the Vaal and Orange rivers. Both republics were appropriately named the Orange Free State and the Transvaal. During their protracted diaspora these Boer communities engaged in bitter conflict with neighbouring African peoples, notably the formidable Zulu nation recently united under their great chief Shaka.

*Sketch map of South Africa, 1879.*

By the mid-nineteenth century this protracted rivalry between these two 'European' groups had reached political stalemate, with the British themselves soon expanding from the Cape to establish, in 1843, a new colony of Natal. With such continued European expansion, African societies became territorially sandwiched between these competing white settler groups. It was an extremely tense situation frequently degenerating into numerous frontier conflicts, notably the nine Cape-Xhosa wars, 1779–1879.

The pressures were intensified during the 1870s by the decision of the British government to confederate all their South African provinces as a means of both reducing financial cost and enhancing overall security. British politician Lord Carnarvon was appointed to spearhead this lengthy and complex political process. The discovery of diamonds in the 1860s had already accelerated British interest in the region and, in 1877, the British annexation of the bankrupt Transvaal Republic engendered a new crisis between the British and many Boer settlers who, while temporarily powerless to prevent the British takeover, saw it as a further encroachment upon their hard-won liberty.

*The Earl of Carnarvon, the primary catalyst behind South African Confederation. (JY)*

For the British the annexation of the Transvaal had precipitated an equally imminent conflict with the adjoining Zulu nation, particularly as they directly inherited a new long border with Zululand and the existing and often bitter Boer territorial disputes with this formidable tribe. Distinguished imperial statesman, Sir Henry Bartle Frere, the newly appointed High Commissioner of South Africa, though not directly responsible for this annexation, was the man now burdened with the heavy task of implementing confederation in the midst of this deadly dual political crisis. For many historians he has nevertheless come to be seen as the arch instigator of the subsequent Anglo-Zulu War.

## Frere's Security Crisis

For the critics of Frere, the subsequent two years were portrayed as a series of provocative moves by him which forced the Zulu into a tragic and ruinous war. He had certainly arrived from India with an awesome reputation as an imperial trouble-shooter and his despatches home to London clearly reflected his firm conviction that the Zulu were at the centre of an African conspiracy to overthrow white rule, or in his own words, conducting a 'simultaneous rising of Kaffirdom against white civilisation'. Zulu violations of the Natal–Zulu border were continually cited by

# OTHER COLONIAL MOTIVES?

More sinister motives lay beneath Frere's acute security problem. Cetshwayo's army of up to 40,000 warriors represented a potential 'virgin' untapped labour pool to be exploited by the local colonial authorities. A break-up of the Zulu empire would certainly serve the needs of white mine owners and farmers and provide a welcome tax yield. In Shepstone's own words: 'Had Cetshwayo's 30, 0000 wariors been in time changed to labourers working for wages, Zululand would now have been a prosperous peaceful country instead of what it now is, a source of perpetual danger to itself and its neighbours.' (RA, Queen Victoria's Journal)

*Sir Henry Bartle Edward Frere, 1815–84, Governor of the Cape and High Commissioner for South Africa since 1877, entrusted with the arduous task of completing Lord Carnarvon's ailing confederation scheme. (JY)*

## FLAWED POLITICAL MASTER?

Arguably Frere's particular misfortune was that his
political superior, Sir Michael Hicks Beach had no
previous experience in colonial administration. Even
his biographer and arch-defender, Lady Hicks Beach,
conceded that he 'had no special knowledge of South
African affairs'. Political historian, C.F. Goodfellow,
observes that it 'was probably his loyalty as much as his
ability which had produced his elevation to the Cabinet
while Chief Secretary for Ireland on November 1876'.
Early on he had admitted to his complete ignorance of
South African affairs and had promised Frere his 'support
and cooperation in your difficult position'. Within twelve
months, however, he was to twice withdraw support for
Frere's Zulu policies, ultimately abandoning him in the
aftermath of the Isandlwana disaster. For some historians
this constituted one of the greatest political betrayals of
the Victorian era. (Sources: Goodfellow, *Britain and South
African Confederation*; Lady V. Hicks Beach, *Life Of Sir
Michael Hicks Beach*)

Frere as evidence of Zulu aggression, as were their alleged links
with hostile foreign powers such as Germany and Russia who
were supplying them with arms. In July 1878 the illegal pursuit
by Zulu forces and brutal murder, by garrotting, of two allegedly
adulterous Zulu women who had fled across the border into British
sovereign territory, finally convinced Frere that the Zulu 'war fever'
had to be 'at once grappled with'. In September 1878, while on
the spot in Natal, he dramatically reported to his superior, Colonial
Secretary Sir Michael Hicks Beach, that the highly vulnerable
25,000 British settlers residing there were now 'slumbering on a
volcano... the Zulus are now quite out of hand'. (Worsfold, *Life of
Sir Bartle Frere*, p.91, Frere to Hicks Beach, 30 September 1878)

However, defenders of Frere, such as myself, while not denying
the racial prejudices shared by much of his generation, have
emphasised Frere's security dilemma as he faced a potentially

*Sir Michael Hicks Beach, Secretary of State for the colonies. (JY)*

## ZULU WAR 'HAWK'

Appointed Secretary for Native Affairs in 1853 and, after 1877, Administrator of the newly annexed Transvaal, Theophilus Shepstone became one of the leading local advocates of war with the Zulu. Born near Bristol in 1817 and the son of a parson, he had originally moved to South Africa in 1820 as a willing recruit for a government-assisted scheme to settle the under-populated Eastern Cape. His approach to African affairs was one of stern paternalism, hence his cultivated self-image as *somsewu* or 'father of whiteness'. His 'Shepstone system', an attempt to subsume the indigenous Zulu *amakhosi* or chiefs into the colonial system as a means of political control and commercial exploitation, reflected a common British approach to African government. He officiated at paramount Zulu Chief Cetshwayo's coronation in 1873 but, as the Zulu elite increasingly clashed with British authority in the mid/late 1870s, he rapidly distanced himself and, like his political superior, Frere, became a leading proponent of the use of force to finally subjugate the Zulu nation.

two-front war from recalcitrant Boer settlers and his new and increasingly truculent Zulu neighbours. The latter could muster an estimated 40,000-strong army. Moreover, in his consequently robust forward policies up to October 1878 Frere was broadly supported by both local colonial officials and by senior colonial officials in London and, most significantly, his inexperienced political superior, the newly appointed Colonial Secretary Sir Michael Hicks Beach.

On his annexation of Pondoland, for instance, one colonial official, Wingfield, wrote of the 'sensible' policy of 'securing a position of influence over Pondoland in the event of war with the Zulus'. With such support from London and the strong backing of his military Commander-in-Chief, Lord Chelmsford and key local Transvaal Administrator Sir Theophilus Shepstone, Frere continued his military build-up against the Zulu during the spring and summer of 1878.

# THE ARMIES

## The British Forces

The preparations for invading Zululand had taken months. In 1879, the British Army remained a largely cumbersome, hierarchical machine, but one which was well used to victory over 'native enemies' in Africa and elsewhere.

But it was an army, due to extended overseas imperial commitments and fighting in extreme alien environments, e.g. the 1874 Ashanti War (in what is now known as Ghana), that often experienced appalling conditions of service, and consequent problems with recruitment. Most rank and file soldiers were recruited from the lowest levels of Victorian urban and rural society, often petty criminals or destitute farm labourers. Before 1870, many recruits had been drawn from Ireland – particularly after the 1840s potato famines – but the great trade depression of the 1870s brought a new influx of urban and rural poor from mainland Britain. By the mid-nineteenth century, service conditions were generally brutal, dull and uncompromising and men were expected to sign on for exceptionally long periods. Up to 1847, men enlisted for life and after that date, for ten years with the option of continuing for twenty-one years to qualify for a pension. On meagre unvarying rations of bread, bully beef and biscuits, the

# A Typical British Soldier

## Rorke's Drift Defender, Private Henry Hook VC (1850–1905)

Private Henry Hook's background epitomised that of many private soldiers in the Victorian army. He was born in the village of Churcham in Gloucestershire on 6 August 1850 and baptised with the Christian name Alfred. However, he adopted his father's name 'Henry'. His occupation began, like many recruits, as a rural labourer. In 1871 his family moved to Monmouth and he worked on farms and around the village of Huntley. He was a well-built youth 1.67m tall.

His motivation for enlistment, a severe personal economic crisis, was typical; he joined up because, at a time of acute agricultural depression, he was experiencing great difficulties paying off the mortgage on his property.

On 13 March 1877 he enlisted at Monmouth and was assigned to the 2nd Battalion, 24th Foot. In February 1878 his battalion was sent to the Cape where he participated in the final defeat of the Xhosa in the 9th Cape Frontier War. His battalion was then deployed to No. 3 Column for the invasion of Zululand in January 1879. His B Company was subsequently assigned to guard the Drift and supply depot at Rorke's Drift. His heroic action in the defence and evacuation of the hospital was to play a significant part in the British victory there.

In 1880, he bought himself out of the army and worked for some years for the British Museum as a cloakroom attendant. In March 1905, he died aged fifty-five of pulmonary tuberculosis, soon after recording his memoirs in the Royal Magazine. His funeral was more spectacular than most, including representatives from twenty-three regiments.

(Sources: Bancroft, *Zulu War VCs*; and Knight and Greaves, *Who's Who in the Zulu War*, Vol. 1)

*Private Hook VC. (JY)*

Victorian soldier eked out an extremely hard existence. Military life consisted of parades and fatigues with training hardly going beyond eternal drill and sporadic gymnastic exercises. In the late Victorian period, out of a gross pay of around seven shillings a week, half would be deducted for food over and above basic rations, and over a tenth of a soldiers pay for laundry services etc.

While the serving conditions for officers were significantly better than the private soldier, their military capabilities were often more suspect. With indifferent pay most officer recruits came from the lower middle classes, often second and third sons from the landed gentry who were excluded from inheritance by the primogeniture system. Class did not ensure quality! Until as recently as 1872, the peculiar anachronistic system of 'purchase of commission' allowed posts to be bought and sold, often for as much as several thousand pounds, a system which was clearly devoid of any meritocratic base.

Between 1856 and 1879, however, a number of significant reforms had improved the overall quality of British Army life and provided it with a more professional base. The graphic despatches of *The Times* reporter William Russell from the Crimea, which detailed horrific service conditions, had exposed many shortcomings in army administration, as did reports of the stirring medical work undertaken by Florence Nightingale. The great Cardwell reforms of 1872 created a much more professional army. The duration of service was shortened, the 'purchase of commission' system was abolished, as were more brutal army practices (although flogging was retained for wartime service).

## Kit: The British and Colonial Forces

Equipment had also improved in the decade preceding the Anglo-Zulu War. In 1871, the army replaced the Enfield percussion rifle (maximum range 1,000 yards) with the new, much more effective, single-shot Martini-Henry breech-loading rifle.

The 'lunger' socket bayonet carried by most of the line regiments in 1879 dated from the 1850s, and was around 21in. long and,

# 'MAN-STOPPER': THE STANDARD MARTINI-HENRY INFANTRY RIFLE

Despatching a heavy .45 calibre lead bullet, the rifle was sighted up to 1,500 yards, although most accurate at a distance of between 300 and 500 yards. The bullet was literally a 'man-stopper' and, at close range, could have a terrible effect on the human body, with the potential to rip both cartilage and bone apart. The rifle action was also much easier. When the lever between the trigger guard was depressed the breech opened. A used round was then extracted and a fresh round inserted in the chamber, and raising the lever closed the breech for firing. The only disadvantage was that the heavy recoil could bruise shoulders and make firing uncomfortable after half an hour or so, while excessive firing could also cause the barrel to overheat, both melting the brass base of the cartridge and sometimes jamming the firing action. These problems did emerge during the battle at Rorke's Drift. More seasoned troops, however, learnt to partly counteract overheating by sowing cowhide around the barrel and stock of the Martini-Henry.

*A Martini-Henry cartouche packet, containing ten cartridges. (RRWM)*

combined with the 4ft rifle length, gave a stabbing reach of over 6ft. As we shall see, this proved to be a distinct advantage during close-quarter combat with the Zulu at Rorke's Drift.

In addition to the rifle and bayonet, each soldier was issued with the standard seventy rounds when going into action. A carbine (shortened) version of the Martini-Henry was also adopted by the British government in April 1871 for use by cavalry.

The 1871 Valise Pattern Equipment proved to be reasonably efficient British Field Dress. It included two white calf leather pouches on each side of the waist-belt, and a black leather 'expense pouch' positioned usually at the back of the belt. Other essential items for the imperial infantry of the 1870s included a wooden water bottle, mess tin, greatcoat and haversack. The uniform was, by contrast, somewhat less practical. The traditional red tunic with facing regimental colours on cuff and collar and secured by regimental buttons was retained, while the blue serge trousers and often poor-quality leather boots completed the infantry Field Dress. As in India, the only real concession to the African heat was the white 'foreign service' helmet displaying the regimental shako badge attached to the front. In South Africa, veterans, in order to make themselves less conspicuous to the enemy, darkened these helmets by staining, usually with tea, coffee or mud. After a few weeks campaigning in the African bush, much of this uniform, particularly the jackets and trousers, were reduced to tatters, and often humorous-looking patchwork variations in dress took over, complimenting the wild beards sported by many of the veterans!

The 24th Foot, comprising the main unit of imperial troops who fought at Rorke's Drift, were an interesting mixture of veterans and relatively novice soldiers. Of the two battalions of the 24th Foot, the 1/24th were the most experienced in African warfare, having arrived at the Cape as early as 1875. They had spent four successive years engaged in largely fluid, short-lived skirmishes with Xhosa rebels in which the new Martini-Henry rifle had been frequently deployed, with maximum destructive effect.

# The Armies

The British regulars were supplemented by numerous colonial irregular units. Local white settler volunteer formations were attached to all five of Chelmsford's columns and as units for defence around the major Natal towns and settlements. Desporting a wide variety of weapons and uniform, contingents such as the Natal Mounted Police and the Buffalo Border Guard comprised a vital adjunct to Chelmsford's regular forces, especially before the arrival of massive reinforcements following the disaster at Isandlwana.

Serving alongside the British regular and white colonial units were the white-officered African levies, notably the Natal Native Contingent (NNC). These African troops were predominantly Zulu-speaking and members of clans closely related to the Zulu, or were refugees or descendants of refugees from Zululand. Some had old

*Natal Native Horse, one of several African irregular units. (JY)*

23

scores to settle with Cetshwayo, and most were recruited by their chiefs and headmen to assist the British regular troops and all-white colonial volunteer units. The contingent consisted of three regiments, the first with three battalions and the second and third with two battalions each. The muster strength of each battalion was around 1,000 men, and each African was issued a blanket and a red cloth headband as a distinguishing mark. Around 100 in each battalion (1 in 10) were armed with often poor quality rifles, the remainder with billhooks or their own assegais and shields. Despite constant drilling, their overall lack of experience and poor equipment ensured that their military value was both marginal and, as we shall see, often unpredictable. At Rorke's Drift the NNC comprised a company of the 2nd Battalion NNC, probably mainly from the aba Thembu polity and commanded by Captain Stevenson (sometimes spelt Stephenson). Estimates of their number vary from 100 to 300. However, their presence at the battle was to prove initially valuable but, in combat terms, ultimately disastrous.

## The British Commanders: Tactics and Logistics

The initial campaign plans of Lord Chelmsford, commander-in-chief of the British invasion forces in January 1879, were simple. Aware of Zulu mobility, the overriding main strategic aim was to force the Zulu Army to battle by striking decisively at the enemy's centre of gravity, the Zulu capital of Ulundi (or more specifically, Cetshwayo's royal kraal or personal home at oNdini). In such a battle superior British volley fire would, it was believed, irrevocably smash the exposed Zulu 'regiments' in the open field. For this purpose, Chelmsford divided his force into five columns each mixing British regular infantry with other colonial units. Three of these would advance from widely separated points on the Zululand border with Natal with two columns held in reserve along the border to protect local white settlers against any Zulu breakthrough. These three attacking columns

# General Lord Chelmsford (1827–1905)

## British Commander-in-Chief

Frederick Augustus Thesiger was born on 31 May 1827 (he succeeded to the title Lord Chelmsford on 5 October 1878). His father was a lawyer and Tory MP. Educated at Eton he purchased a commission in the Rifle Brigade. He served in the Crimea in a non-active staff duty capacity and later saw limited action in the mopping-up operations during the Indian Mutiny in 1859. He was also involved in the Abyssinian campaign of 1868 as Deputy Adjutant-General. Later as the ADC to the Queen and Adjutant-General of India he married, had four sons and met the Governor of Bombay Sir Henry Bartle Frere, a man with whose political fate he was destined to be closely entwined.

After returning to serve at Aldershot he accepted his first independent active service command for thirty-four years in South Africa in 1878. He played a key role in the final stages of the Cape Xhosa war, remembered as a commanding, robust personality with a tall spare frame, black beard and bushy eyebrows. As a tactician he was considered competent but uninspired. In South Africa he renewed his acquaintance with Frere and fully shared his views on Confederation and imperial security.

On 11 January 1879 Chelmsford led the invasion of Zululand and achieved his first minor success against the stronghold of the border chief Sihayo the next day. After transport delays due to the terrible terrain he reached the campsite of Isandlwana. Here he was much criticised for failing to secure the camp defences and for allowing his forces to be divided as he left the camp in a fruitless search for the main Zulu army. He was consequently at least 12 miles away when his weakened garrison was destroyed. The stupendous British victory at Rorke's Drift that same day, whilst providing an enormous fillip to British morale, was ultimately overshadowed by this terrible defeat. Despite the shock of a defeat and ignoring advice to retire on health grounds, he persevered with a renewed offensive in March 1879. He secured a victory at Gingindlovu and he finally broke Cetshwayo's regiments at the battle of Ulundi on 4 July 1879. (Source: Greaves and Knight, *Who's Who in the Zulu War 1879*, Vol. 1, pp.54–60)

*Lieutenant General Frederick Augustus Thesiger (Lord Chelmsford). (KR)*

in a strange replication of Zulu tactics would be deployed in a slowly enveloping pincer movement aimed towards the Zulu capital. No. 4 Column, the northern most on Chelmsford's left, was commanded by Colonel Charles Pearson and comprised nearly 5,000 men The main thrust of the invasion centred on No. 3 Column, led by Colonel Richard Glyn, comprising just under 4,700 men, which was poised to strike directly at Ulundi via Rorke's Drift and Isandlwana. This column was accompanied by Chelmsford himself. An early decisive blow by any of these three columns was considered essential.

Already confident of his military superiority in open battle, much of Chelmsford's pre-invasion preparations were focused on the immense logistical or supply and transport problems presented by such a difficult country lacking in any form of road.

Transport was a herculean, almost nightmarish task. Chelmsford had to shift 1,500 tons of tents, cooking utensils, food, rifle and artillery ammunition and medical stores via 18ft ox wagons hauled by eighteen-to-twenty-strong oxen or mule teams, all of which were highly susceptible to sickness or accident.

Hitherto, comfortable in their strategy and sure of success, the British forces were left reeling by their unexpected defeat at Isandlwana, making their defence of the Rorke's Drift garrison crucial to their overall campaign.

## The Zulu Army in 1879

The Zulu Army, once famously described by Sir Bartle Frere as 'a nation of celibate man-slaying gladiators' owed their allegiance to King Cetshwayo Ka Mpande, who had become the Zulu paramount chief after the death of his father, Mpande, in 1872. On this date, the forty-year-old Cetshwayo became ruler of some 300,000 people, most of whom inhabited the territory between the Thukela (Tugela) and Mzinyathi (Buffalo) rivers and the valley of the Phongola.

# King Cetshwayo Ka Mpande (1832–1884)

## Overall Commander of the Zulu Armies

Cetshwayo, paramount chief of the Zulu during the 1879 Anglo-Zulu War was born at emLambongweya in 1832 and was the son of Prince Mpande Ka Senzangakhona. When his father concluded an unholy alliance with the Boers in order to contest King Dingane for the Zulu throne, Cetshwayo began his slow but steady rise to power. Around 1850, he enrolled into the uThulwana *ibutho*. In 1852 Cetshwayo saw his first action during a raid against the rival Swazi tribe. His superior fighting skills gave him significant prestige.

As Cetshwayo's influence and ambitions rapidly grew even his father became concerned, and began to favour Mbuyazi, another of his twenty-nine sons. The inevitable rivalry ended in bloodshed in 1856 when Cetshwayo's superior 20,000-strong *impi* inflicted a crushing defeat of Mbuyazi's forces of 7,000 warriors on the Thukela River during which Mbuyazi himself was killed.

After his father's death in 1872, Cetshwayo was crowned king in August 1873. Cetshwayo then proceeded to construct a new royal homestead at oNdini or Ulundi. The next seven years were troublesome times as he faced renewed pressures on his lands from Boer settlers and internal challenges to his royal authority.

After 1877 and the annexation of the Transvaal, Cetshwayo confronted British authority, only partially alleviated by the pro-Zulu findings of the Boundary Commission. Sir Bartle Frere's perseverance with an ultimatum on 11 December 1878 precipitated a final crisis for his kingdom. He remained in a defensive posture but when the British invaded and destroyed his favourite border chief's Sihayo's kraal, he committed his armies to an all out offensive.

The Isandlwana victory was marred both by the heavy losses (he subsequently commented 'an assegai has been thrust into the belly of the nation') and the almost simultaneous defeats at Rorke's Drift and iNyezane.

In March 1878, Cetshwayo faced further defeats at Gingindlovu and Khambula. With the British rejecting last-minute concessions, he was finally defeated by Chelmsford's 5,000-strong force at oNdini on 4 July 1879. (Source: Greaves and Knight, *Who's Who in the Zulu War*, Vol. 2, p.127)

*Cetshwayo in traditional dress. (JY)*

## Kit: The Zulu

Individual Zulu regiments were mainly distinguished by their shield colouring, although some regimental differentiations had apparently been significantly diluted by the time of Cetshwayo's reign. One 'great distinction' remained, however, that between the married and unmarried regiments, 'the former... obliged to shave the crown of the head and to wear a ring made of hemp and coated with a hardened paste of gum and grease; they also carried white shields while the unmarried regiments wore their hair naturally and had coloured shields – black or reddish'. (War Office, Precis, p.87)

At Rorke's Drift the four regiments of the attacking Undi Corps were predominantly head-ringed married men, the married uThulwana and iNdlondlo carrying white shields with small patches of red while the younger unmarried iNdluyengwe were still equipped with black shields encompassing large white patches on the bottom half. The married uDloko, by contrast, desported either red-brown shields, patterned with white, or white shields.

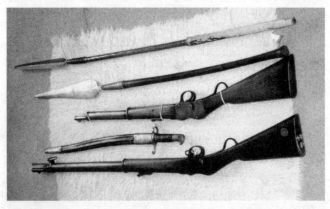

*A collection of British and Zulu weaponry. Note the potential stabbing length of the Martini-Henry rifle (bottom) once the bayonet is attached. The shorter stabbing assegai is a modern replica. (EY)*

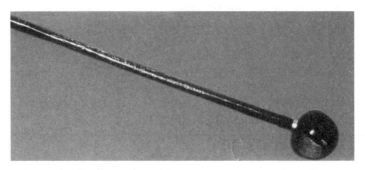

*The Zulu knobkerrie which Chard recovered from the Rorke's Drift battlefield. (Jane Woodward/Chard family collection)*

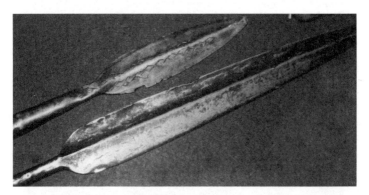

*The heads of two Zulu spears/assegais, discovered after the Rorke's Drift battle by Lieutenant Colonel J. Audley-Lloyd. (RRWM)*

*A broken (later inscribed) shield shaft, recovered by Lieutenant Bromhead from the battlefield after the siege of Rorke's Drift. (RRWM)*

For battle, Zulu warriors usually wore minimal clothing, consisting of a small loin cloth or, less frequently, some minimal ostrich feather head-dress or other ornamentation.

Mobilisation for war was rapid, the king informing the various *indunas* (commanders) by runners who then called up the *amabutho* from their specific *amakhanda*. From there, the regiments would converge and congregate at the king's kraal at oNdini.

Zulu battle practices were ruthless and uncompromising. Male prisoners were never or rarely taken, women only as booty and the objective, as in Shaka's day, was to totally annihilate the opposing enemy forces. The prevailing Zulu tactic for close-quarter battle, originated and perfected by Shaka, was to hook the opponent's shield to the left and deliver the assegai thrust to the exposed chest.

# THE ZULU MILITARY SYSTEM

The core of the Zulu military system originated by Shaka in the 1820s rested upon the age set units known as *amabutho* (singular *ibutho*). Under this system, teenage Zulu boys, generally aged between fourteen and eighteen, would firstly be assembled and concentrated at military kraals called *amakhanda* (singular *ikhanda*). Here they would be inculcated in basic military and economic skills, including cattle herding, shield and spear techniques. When sufficient numbers were gathered together at various kraals, all would be brought before the king and formally adopted into a regiment or *ibutho* with orders to build a new *ikhanda*. Those who in this way gave their political allegiance to the king were then given the right to occupy and work his land and even retain parts of the fruits of their labour. By 1879, there were twenty-seven *amakhanda* in Zululand and thirteen based on the Mahlabathini Plain surrounding Cetshwayo's capital oNdini. The *amabutho* would perform a number of functions or services for the king, aside from military service in major wars. These could include raiding or policing operations, such as collecting fines from offenders.

*Zulu warrior groups. Zulu boys would be taught basic economic and military skills at military kraals, known as* 'amakhanda'. *(AB)*

The Zulu armoury was supplemented by significant numbers of mostly obsolete European firearms, such as muzzle-loading Enfield 'Brown Bess' or 'Tower' muskets. These were acquired mainly from Portuguese traders in the Delagoa Bay area, fuelling Sir Bartle Frere's fears of conspiratorial links between the Zulu and rival European powers.

## The Zulu Commanders: Tactics and Logistics

Zulu battle tactics, again based on the innovative ideas of the Zulu military genius Shaka, hinged upon the rapid encircling and enveloping formation known as *'impondo zankomo'* ('beasts horns'). The Zulu units generally comprising the younger and more able bodied *amabutho*, occupied the two fast-moving left

# A typical Zulu Warrior

The life of a Zulu warrior was both physically extremely robust and also deeply spiritual. His entire boyhood would be focused on the veldt, usually tending cattle. This outdoor existence would both toughen his body and provide him with extensive knowledge of local terrain. He would become expert in herding, hunting and fighting skills. Walking or paced running over long distances of up to 40 or even 50 miles was common by adulthood. His diet would consist of at least two meals a day, the food including boiled or toasted maize cobs, boiled sweet potatoes, served from a common food bowl shared by each member of the family. Meat was considered a luxury, especially beef, for Zulu status was measured by the number of cattle they owned.

These martial skills were reinforced by complete submission to the authority of their all powerful elders or *amakhosi*. Any deviation from unquestioning obedience could lead to a range of severe penalties including banishment or even death. At puberty the young boys were bonded together into age groups based on military kraals run by *indunas* responsible for order and discipline, where they were taught the elementary skills of combat. Adolescent Zulus were formed into regiments and placed in military kraals. Their essentiallly feudal duties could range from simple policing to all out war.

This intensely physical world was matched by a deeply spiritual dimension, populated by spirits of their dead ancestors. Their ancestral spirits, *amadlozi*, kept a watchful eye, intervening to bring either good luck or disaster. Hence the importance of rituals and ceremony throughout their lives especially the up to three-day ceremonies conducted before battle. In the words of historian Ian Knight, it was a life conducted in a 'state of physical and psychological bondage'. Such physical virtues and deep unshakable spiritual beliefs made the Zulu warrior a formidable enemy for the British to contend with. (Sources: Knight, *Zulu Rising* and Laband, *Rise and Fall of the Zulu Kingdom*)

*A classic, accurate engraving of a Zulu charge. Note the deployment of muskets alongside traditional spears and assegais. (EY)*

and right wings, 'horns' or 'claws' of the crescent-shaped mass with the aim of rapidly surrounding the enemy on each flank. Meanwhile, a powerful body of the more experienced *amabutho*, comprising the 'chest' of the beast, would attack and distract the enemy head-on, with a reserve or 'loins' deployed behind as reinforcements. Strict discipline was paramount, the 'loins' often kept seated with their backs to the action to discourage premature intervention.

For traditional and spiritual reasons Cetshwayo himself was unable to undertake direct field or active command. The Zulu high command structure largely consisted of Cetshwayo's favourite *indunas*, who had previously displayed conspicuous loyalty at times of crisis, notably the bitter and bloody succession war of 1856 or in the many confrontations with the Boer enemy, or, who were closely related to his royal clan or, who satisfied both criteria. Rorke's Drift commander Prince Dabulamanzi amply fulfilled the criteria for royal connection.

Such strategies were not necessarily effective against heavily fortified positions, as shown between the differing outcomes at Isandlwana, where the British allowed themselves to be outflanked and overstretched on a more open field, and the defence of a heavily barricaded Rorke's Drift, where the Zulu were unable to achieve the same success.

# THE DAYS BEFORE BATTLE

In October 1878, as the British military build-up continued, Frere's war policy against the Zulu was suddenly and totally undermined by two 'bombshell' telegrams and despatches from Colonial Secretary Hicks Beach which effectively vetoed war with the Zulu. A trade and agricultural depression and, in particular, the looming threat from Russia in the Near East and an imminent war in Afghanistan had turned the British Prime Minister Disraeli and his Cabinet away from the prospect of yet another costly colonial war.

Frere, as his defenders point out, was placed in an impossible strategic dilemma. The official vetoing of his own war plans and local military intelligence reports of reciprocal hostile Zulu activity against his highly vulnerable 200-mile Natal and Transvaal frontiers, combined with the slowness of communication with London, meant that he was now extremely vulnerable to rapid pre-emptive strikes by Cetshwayo's armies or equally worse, by hostile Boer commandos. He later wrote:

> It was a simple solution, risking a Zulu war at once or incurring the risk of still worse, a Zulu war a few months later, preceded by a Boer rebellion.
>
> St Aldwyn/Hicks Beach papers, Frere to Hicks Beach,
> 25 April 1879

# THE RUSSIAN THREAT/ AFGHANISTAN DIVERSIONS

The obsession of the Disraeli government (1874–80) with the Russian threat in the Near East and Central Asia during late 1878 had a major diversionary and arguably detrimental impact on their policy towards the Zulu 'problem'. In October and early November 1878 it was the ongoing crisis and the eventual outbreak of war in Afghanistan, designed to counter Russian influence in Kabul and possible invasion of India, which largely prompted Prime Minister Disraeli and his Colonial Secretary to radically change their earlier policy of general support for Frere's policies and to veto any prospect of war with the Zulu.

However, the subsequent two decisive victories achieved against Afghan forces at Ali Masjid and Peiwar Khotal in late November and early December 1878, prompted the government into a further *volte face* and a sudden reversal of their opposition to a potential Zulu War. But that this support was only to be contingent upon another 'cheap and successful victory' was soon to be graphically evident in the cynical political abandonment and condemnation of Frere after news of the unexpected and costly disaster at Isandlwana on 22 January 1879 .(Source: Yorke, P*laying the Great Game*, Chapters 4 and 5)

On this basis Frere felt compelled to both exceed his instructions and to proceed with an ultimatum to Cetshwayo and the Zulu nation. Astonishingly it was an act of disobedience which while initially chastised was, a few weeks later, to be conveniently ignored by his superiors in London. Within weeks of his war veto and condemnation of Frere's proposals for an ultimatum, Hicks Beach suddenly 'reversed his reversal'. The reason was both cynical and expedient. Early and unexpected British victories in Afghanistan in November and early December 1878 had created scope for an anticipated short and cheap war with the Zulu or, as Hicks Beach himself put it:

*The swotting of a 'Zulu wasp' by the British lion. This 1879* Punch *cartoon graphically shows that the Zulu threat was only one of several problems besetting the hard-pressed Disraeli government.*

there is, I hope, a good prospect of the war being short and successful like the Afghan campaign... so that on the whole, although Frere's policy, especially in the matter of cost, is extremely inconvenient to us, I am sanguine as to its success and think we shall be able, without much difficulty, to defend its principles here.

St Aldwyn/ Hicks Beach Papers, Hicks Beach to Disraeli,
13 January 1879

As we shall see, news received on 11 February 1879 of the totally unexpected and crushing defeat of Chelmsford's main garrison at Isandlwana was to change all this. Frere's subsequent political recall and censure, his enduring and understandable sense of betrayal and his protracted defence of his actions, was to make the Rorke's Drift victory an event of considerably enhanced political, as well as military, significance.

# The Descent to War

Events moved swiftly from Frere's initial issuing of his ultimatum on 11 December 1878, calling for, among other things, the immediate dismantlement of the Zulu military system and complete submission to British 'supervision'. Predictably, Cetshwayo was not prepared to accept such terms and allowed the ultimatum to expire. On 11 January 1879, the first British troops crossed over the Natal border into Zululand.

Lord Chelmsford and Colonel Glyn's No. 3 Column launched their incursion with little or no knowledge of the whereabouts of the Zulu forces, whereas Cetshwayo's spies had already fed back details of the composition and likely movements of the British Army to the waiting Zulus. The British crossing of the Buffalo River was a foretaste of the logistical difficulties that the army was to face during the Zulu campaign. It was unopposed, however, which was taken as a good omen.

Indeed, within twenty-four hours of the crossing, a British reconnaissance force, led by Major John Dartnell, located Chief Sihayo's homestead and launched their attack. But, it was not as straightforward as they had anticipated, the Zulu initially proved to be steadfast in their resistance and it was only the deadly fire of the Martini-Henry rifles that ensured British success.

It is commonly held that this seemingly insignificant skirmish at Sihayo's kraal prompted a much more belligerent response from the hitherto recalcitrant Cetshwayo, who is reported saying on reviewing his troops:

> I am sending against the white man, the white man who has invaded Zululand and driven away your cattle. You are to go against the column at Ishyane [Rorke's Drift] and drive it back into Natal and go on up the Drakensburg.
>
> H.A. Hallam Parr, *Sketch of the Zulu and Kafir Wars*, pp.184–5

It was clear that Cetshwayo was now ready to wage war.

# The Battle of Isandlwana, 22 January 1879

Amidst ominous intelligence reports about Zulu activity, the column pushed on further into Zululand. As feared, after the heavy rains of late 1878/early 1879, it was a tortuous journey – taking over a week to cover the 10 miles by wagon track to the next campsite at Isandlwana. The whole column, and in particular the 24th, were 'worked hard', the worst obstacle being 'low lying bits of track on soft soil made swampy by springs and wet weather into which the heavy wagons sank axle deep'. (Hallam Parr, *Sketches*, p.185)

The organisation and layout of the No. 3 Centre Column camp beneath the ominous sphinx-like crag of Isandlwana on 20 January 1879, the first one of several designated staging posts on the road to oNdini or Ulundi, immediately revealed a number of defensive vulnerabilities. While it was located close by wood and water supplies, Chelmsford chose neither to entrench the camp or laager (form a defensive circle) for his 100-odd wagons. At the subsequent Court of Inquiry into the Isandlwana disaster, it was pointed out that the predominantly rocky ground was unsuited for digging and that the wagons had to be kept un-harnessed and mobile in order to sustain the essential 20-mile circuitous return journey between the campsite and the main supply base at Rorke's Drift. Thus logistical imperatives had already severely compromised the defensive capabilities of the Isandlwana garrison. Moreover, it was argued that both laagering and entrenchment were not justified by the designated temporary nature of the campsite.

The whole camp extended to about a 1,300-yard frontage, protected only to the rear by the crag and lacking any physical protection to the front or flanks. It was a potential defensive nightmare with the two ammunition wagons of the battalions positioned as much as half a mile apart. The garrison's defences were also severely compromised by the restricted use of vedettes (mounted sentries) and cavalry in general who, until the fateful morning of 22 January, were not deployed much beyond the Nqutu Heights and were, therefore, unable detect the arrival and concealment of the main Zulu Army.

For Chelmsford, however, the main problem remained; how to locate precisely and bring to battle the main Zulu Army now reliably reported to have departed from the Zulu capital several days earlier. It was in obsessively trying to solve this problem that several more major errors were committed.

On 21 January a reconnaissance force led by Major Dartnell blundered into a sizeable Zulu force, 15 miles into the Hlazakazi hills. In the view of some historians it was possibly a Zulu feint but it too easily confirmed Chelmsford's expectations, and, afraid that the main Zulu Army would elude him, he (in hindsight) rashly committed roughly half his force to offensive action. Chelmsford had unknowingly split his forces without precise knowledge of the whereabouts of his enemy. In the early hours of Wednesday 22 January he departed leaving approximately 1,700 British troops and African allies to guard the main camp. Command was invested in an inexperienced officer, Brevet Lieutenant Colonel Henry Pulleine with orders to 'draw in your line of defence'. This order was fatally compromised by two key events.

Firstly, the warriors encountered the day before were not the main Zulu Army; this had already earlier deployed across Chelmsford's front and unbeknown to either Chelmsford or Pulleine, lay concealed in the Ngwebeni Valley, 5 miles away and dangerously close to the main camp's left flank. While Chelmsford spent the morning fruitlessly searching for the enemy up to 12 miles away, scouts from Colonel Durnford's force which had arrived in camp later that fateful morning, suddenly stumbled into the main Zulu Army. The surprise was mutual; the Zulu commanders had not planned to attack the camp until the next day but, now exposed, they launched a massive assault on the site.

Secondly, Pulleine had already overextended his defensive lines, eventually deploying around half of his six companies of 1/24th and 2/24th regulars to a forward position up to a mile from the camp, possibly in deference to Durnford, who, on arrival, had requested support for his reconnaissance mission. Virtually all the British garrison officers had therefore fatally underestimated their enemy as the over 20,000-strong Zulu *impi* advanced in their traditional 'horns of the bull' formation. Although the regular infantry briefly held the Zulu centre or 'chest' by sustained volley fire, they were inevitably outflanked; a dire situation arguably exacerbated by a failing ammunition supply. Despite evidence of gallant efforts to regroup, the lines were broken up and the vast majority of the men were overwhelmed and annihilated by the rapidly encircling Zulu horns. Around 1,300 of the garrison were killed including all the 600 mainly 1/24th Foot regular infantry. Only a small number, primarily NNC and mounted NNH African auxiliaries and barely sixty white men, including only five imperial officers, escaped via 'Fugitives Drift', most frantically heading towards the nearest tiny British outposts at Helpmekaar and Rorke's Drift.

Soon after midday, in the aftermath of the Isandlwana massacre the over 4,000-strong Zulu Reserve, the Undi Corps,

*Isandlwana after the massacre. A lone sentry guards a wrecked wagon, surrounded by the detritus of the battle (May–June 1879). (RMAS)*

# Prince Dabulamanzi Ka Mpande (c. 1840–1886)

## Commander-in-Chief of the Zulu *Impi* at Rorke's Drift

The birth date of Prince Dabulamanzi remains uncertain but we know he was connected to the same royal house as his older brother, Prince Cetshwayo, and that he was enrolled in an *ibutho*, the uDloko, which was established around 1858. By all accounts he was a confident and self-assertive youth and he predictably supported Cetshwayo during the bloody 1856 royal succession war.

Much of his youth was spent in the coastal region of Zululand. Here, Dabulamanzi learnt to ride and became familiar with European culture. The renowned traveller, Bertram Mitford described him as:

> … a fine looking man… stoutly built and large-limbed like most of his royal brethren. He is light in colour even for a Zulu, and has a high intellectual forehead clear eyes and handsome, regular features, with jet-black beard and moustache.

During the 1878 political crisis with the British, he urged compliance with British demands but, later, loyally committed himself to the cause when war eventually broke out.

With his regiment he took part in the great advance towards the main British camp at Isandlwana. Although he held no official command, the wounding of the official commander, Zibhebu, during the battle, combined with his domineering personality, led to him assuming *de facto* command of the Undi Corps.

From here Dabulamanzi went on to attack Rorke's Drift despite Cetshwayo's explicit orders not to cross into British Natal. Despite his later well-publicised statement, that having been denied action at Isandlwana, he wanted to 'wash the spears of his boys', his wider strategic objectives remain mysterious and controversial. The attack there ended in defeat and personal humiliation for the somewhat reckless and relatively combat-inexperienced Dabulamanzi.

He continued to support Cetshwayo throughout the rest the war.

Following the turmoil of the post-Zulu War settlement, his forces clashed with local Boers in north-eastern Zululand. In the ensuing skirmishes in September 1886, he was shot dead by a Boer commando named Paul van de Berg. This was a tragic end for a brave, if flawed Zulu commander. (Source: Greaves and Knight, *Who's Who in the Zulu War*, Vol. 2, p.137)

*Prince Dabulamanzi with some of his retainers. Note the prevalence of firearms. (HPL/RMAS)*

largely spectators to the battle, detached itself from the victorious main Zulu Army in order to launch an attack on Rorke's Drift itself. In the absence of their highly capable and experienced commander, Zibhebhu kaMaphitha, wounded earlier in the battle, the impetuous commander of the uDloko Regiment, Prince Dabulamanzi, had by virtue of his royal pedigree and domineering personality, immediately taken overall command of the corps. His avowed objective, contrary to Cetshwayo's strict orders not to attack Natal, was now to gain battle honours belatedly and 'wash the spears of his boys' in the blood of the vastly outnumbered and unsuspecting group of British soldiers garrisoning this remote outpost.

# THE BATTLEFIELD:
## WHAT ACTUALLY HAPPENED?

> Nothing will happen and I shall be back again this evening – early.
>
> Major Spalding to Chard, c.midday, 22 January 1879

## Calm Before the Storm

Commanding officer Henry Spalding's blissful ignorance of this imminent threat to his command was shared by everyone within Rorke's Drift on that terrible 'Black Wednesday' morning. As the fateful day dawned the scene was peaceful and uneventful; in short, just another routine day. Private Henry Hook, 2nd Battalion, 24th Regiment, laconically recalled, 'we were all knocking about and I was making tea for the sick, as I was hospital cook at the time'. (Hook Account, Holme, *Silver Wreath*, p.63) Private Frederick Hitch was engaged in similar duties, brewing up for his mates in the company tented area outside the buildings. (Hitch Account, ibid., p.62) Indeed for many men there was a profound sense of boredom, even vacuum, as with Durnford's early morning departure, the hustle and bustle caused by hundreds of men of the doomed No. 3 Column passing through, had so abruptly ended. Surgeon Major James Henry Reynolds was particularly miffed:

*Rorke's Drift, the mission station before the attack. Witt's house, which served as a hospital, is on the right; his chapel, used as a storehouse, is on the left. (JY)*

*Private Frederick Hitch VC. (RRWM)*

I remember... my feeling of disappointment when Lord Chelmsford marched away with his army and left me with about 100 other men to sit still and bite the bullet of inactivity at Rorke's Drift. There was no fighting for us, no doctoring for me; the army moved away to gain glory and we sat down in what Lord Halsbury would call a sort of base, to envy the other chaps their chances!

'How VC's are won; A tale of Rorke's Drift
(told by its last VC)' USA, 1903 AMCM

Private Hook expressed similar emotions:

> Everything was perfectly quiet at Rorke's Drift, particularly after
> the Column [Durnford's force] had left – not a soul suspected
> that only a dozen miles away the very men we had said
> 'goodbye' and 'good luck' to were either dead or standing,
> back to back in a last fierce fight with the Zulus.
>
> Holme, *Silver Wreath*, Hook Account, p.63

Colour Sergeant Frank Bourne recalled his palpable sense of
frustration and despair, especially after apparently witnessing the
first successful British action at Sihayo's kraal:

> One Company was left behind at Rorke's Drift to guard the
> Hospital, stores and the pontoons at the Drift on the Buffalo
> river. This was my company and at the time I was bitterly
> disappointed. We saw the main column under Lord Chelmsford
> engage the enemy at once and I watched the action, along with
> my four Sergeants from a little hill by Rorke's Drift. Then we saw
> them move on again and they disappeared.
>
> Holme, *Silver Wreath*, Bourne Account, p.59

By contrast Acting Assistant Commissary Walter Dunne simply
felt isolated:

> Our post at Rorke's Drift seemed silent and lonely after they had
> left; but we expected to join them soon and to hear of some
> fierce but successful fight with the enemy.
>
> *Waggoner*, April 1991

Two officers, Lieutenants Chard and Smith-Dorrien, were at least
busy early on that fateful morning. Smith-Dorrien had arrived
back at the Drift just before dawn, bearing the ill-fated message
from Lord Chelmsford which ordered Durnford and his several
100-strong African auxiliary force to move up to reinforce the

main camp at Isandlwana. Apparently 'hearing heavy guns over at Isandlwana,' Smith-Dorrien himself decided to return, riding the perilous 10 miles back to the doomed camp where he arrived at about 8am. Before he departed he briefly delayed to commence the erection of a 15ft-high 'gallows' for making much-needed bullock-hide ropes and, anticipating a ' big fight', took the precaution of borrowing eight revolver rounds from Lieutenant 'Gonny' Bromhead. It proved to be a very wise decision; it was to be a 'very big fight' for all three officers on that momentous day.

Chard was also busy that morning. The night before he had received an order from No. 3 Column headquarters, 'to say that the men of the Royal Engineers who had lately arrived were to proceed to the camp at Isandlwana at once' (although he 'had received no orders himself'). With the permission of the Commanding Officer Major Spalding, Chard had accordingly put his three Royal Engineer sappers and their full accoutrements into an empty wagon, but as the wagon slowed up, with the difficult terrain, he rode ahead in advance. On his arrival at the camp, probably at around 10am, Chard experienced the first sense of unease. Borrowing a 'very good' field glass from an un-named 24th Regiment NCO, he observed the Zulu enemy moving on the distant hills 'apparently in great force'. This chilling sight alarmed him sufficiently to postulate that the Zulu might sweep round and 'make a dash at the ponts'. Chard hurriedly left the camp. A quarter of a mile out of the camp, on the return road to Rorke's Drift, he met the doomed Colonel Durnford and his mounted force, with whom he left his three men, now sadly destined to die that afternoon alongside Durnford. On his return to Rorke's Drift, Chard was issued with his 'Order for the Day' from his commanding officer which interestingly survived intact 'from the fact of it being carried in my pocket during the fight'.

# Lieutenant John Rouse Merriot Chard RE VC (1847–1897)

## Commander, Rorke's Drift Garrison

Lieutenant John Chard was born at Box Hill, near Plymouth, Devon on 21 December 1847. Chard was educated at Plymouth New Grammar School and the Royal Military Academy, Woolwich.

In 1868 he was commissioned as a lieutenant in the Corps of Royal Engineers. After serving in Bermuda to build fortifications in late 1878 he was deployed to South Africa with the 5th Company, Royal Engineers. After arriving in Durban on 5 January 1879 he was sent up country to join Lord Chelmsford's No. 3, Centre Column.

To ease the appalling transport conditions, Lieutenant Chard was sent forward to Rorke's Drift on 19 January. Here he was engaged repairing the flat-bottomed ponts which had been badly damaged during prolonged use by Chelmsford's transiting troops. On the early morning of 22 January, Chard was ordered to move his sappers up to the newly established main camp at Isandlwana, but, whilst travelling there he was recalled back to Rorke's Drift by his commanding officer, Major Spalding, and he was forced to leave his unit. Later that morning Spalding departed in order to seek out reinforcements from the nearby British base at Helpmakaar; he left Chard in charge.

Hours later Chard was faced with the greatest test of his career as, in the aftermath of the Isandlwana massacre that same day, up to 4,000 Zulu of the Undi Corps attacked his post. In the ensuing battle, Chard performed magnificently and his leadership qualities and tactical skills were to prove critical to its successful defence.

John Chard's professional career flourished in the post-war years – matched by his private audiences with Queen Victoria and a hero's welcome in his home town. The people of Plymouth presented him

with various gifts, including a Sword of Honour. He died on 1 November 1897, aged forty-nine. Queen Victoria had not forgotten her Rorke's Drift hero and sent both a Diamond Jubilee medal and a laurel wreath to his funeral, inscribed, 'A mark of admiration and regard for a brave soldier, from his sovereign'. (Sources: Bancroft, *The Zulu War VCs*; Greaves and Knight, *Who's Who in the Zulu War 1879*, Vol. 1)

*Lieutenant John Rouse Merriot Chard VC, Commander of Rorke's Drift. (KR)*

Camp Rorke's Drift

22 January 1879: Camp morning orders

No.1   The force under Lieutenant Colonel Durnford, RE, having departed, a guard of six privates and one NCO will be furnished by the detachment 2/24th Regiment on the ponts.

A Guard of 50 armed natives will likewise be furnished by Captain Stevenson's detachment at the same spot – the ponts will be invariably drawn over to the Natal side at night. This duty will cease on the arrival of Captain Rainforth's company, 1/24th Regiment.

No.2   accordance with Para 19, Regulations for Field Forces in South Africa, Captain Rainforth's company, 1/24th Regiment, will entrench itself on the spot assigned to it by Column Orders Para-dated-

Spalding, Major Commanding.

Holme, *Silver Wreath*, Chard Account, p.49

*The ponts on the Buffalo River at Rorke's Drift. The mission station is a quarter of a mile inland to the right. (JY)*

## The Battlefield: What Actually Happened?

In the event, Rainforth's company failed to arrive and a concerned Chard, aware of the consequent vulnerability of the ponts, guarded by only seven men, and possibly the lack of entrenchment, spoke to Spalding. Spalding subsequently decided to track down the missing company himself in the vicinity of Helpmekaar. Just before riding away, he paused to establish with Chard the command situation in his absence:

> Which of you is senior, you or Bromhead: I said, 'I don't know'
> – he went back into his tent, looked at an Army List and
> coming back said 'I see you are senior, so you will be in charge,
> although, of course, nothing will happen, and I shall be back
> again this early evening'.
>
> <div align="right">Holme, <i>Silver Wreath</i>, Chard Account, p.49</div>

For some, Major Spalding's absence has been interpreted as at best negligence and at worse desertion of his post. Clearly however, Spalding, ignorant of the massacre of his colleagues at No. 3 Column camp site, could not anticipate in any way an attack on his post by up to one-fifth of that attacking Zulu force.

In order to analyse the battle for Rorke's Drift it is convenient to divide the action into four distinct stages. Firstly, the frantic preparations and initial assaults during which the Zulu regiments attacked the post from the rear. Secondly the main battle when, under severe defensive fire, the main Zulu regiments swung round to focus their main attack on the front walls. Thirdly, the nadir or lowest point for the British defenders when as Zulu snipers caused serious casualties and the first Zulu elements penetrated the weaker hospital defences and set fire to the hospital, the British were forced to withdraw to the inner 'biscuit box' perimeter and surviving patients had to be evacuated. This was the closest the Zulu came to victory. Fourthly the final ordeal, the bitter but inconclusive fight for the storehouse and cattle kraal areas, when the British were forced to retreat a little further and consolidate around their final redoubt position where the Zulu mounted their more sporadic closing overnight assaults. This ended with the early morning arrival of Chelmsford's relief column.

## Phase 1: Battle Preparations and the Initial Zulu Assaults

| | | |
|---|---|---|
| | c.12.30–2.30pm | Various Rorke's Drift garrison staff hear sounds of heavy guns firing from direction of Isandlwana. African warriors initially and, as it proved, mistakenly thought to be friendly NNC, seen approaching the Buffalo or Mzinyathi River |
| | c.3–3.30pm | First fugitives from the Isandlwana disaster filter into the Rorke's Drift post and Chard's river camp. Chard returns to the post. With official confirmation of the Isandlwana defeat the garrison, on Dalton's instigation, abandon evacuation plans and commence building defences |
| 22 January 1879 | 3.30–3.45pm | Group of approx. 100 NNH arrive at Rorke's Drift and are deployed behind Shiyane hill to reconnoitre and frustrate or delay Zulu advance |
| | 4.20pm | First shots of the battle. The NNH abandon position and retreat in the direction of Helpmekaar. The approx. 100–300 NNC, demoralised by this spectacle also take flight |
| | c.4.30pm | The first Zulus, approx. 600 men of the iNdluyengwe ibutho, arrive and attack the rear of the post but are checked by intense volley and enfilading fire and deploy round to the front of the post |

As black as hell and as thick as grass…

> Hall, Natal Mounted Police, Lugg Account,
> Emery, *Red Soldier*, p.132

I myself had given up all hopes of escaping…

> Sergeant G Smith, 2/24th Regiment, Holme,
> *Silver Wreath*, p.61

## The Battlefield: What Actually Happened?

By around 12.30pm, as Chard returned to his tent by the river to both write letters home and indulge in a 'comfortable' lunch, three other members of the garrison, Surgeon Reynolds, Chaplain Smith and Reverend Witt, the resident missionary, were abruptly alerted by the sound of heavy guns. After a conversation, Reynolds remarked, 'if we can't fight… at least we can look on'. The three men then climbed the Oskarsberg or Shiyane Hill, gazed across the Buffalo River but were disappointed to discover that Isandlwana crag (5 miles away) 'shut our view from the scene of the action'. Nevertheless, the report of three or more big guns was 'distinctly audible' with 'a quarter of an hour's interval between each if them'. The timing of their excursion clearly coincided with the height of the battle for the Isandlwana campsite. Within an hour, a potentially more ominous sight greeted their eyes as 'a large body of natives' 'scrambling about' the slope of Isandlwana 'headed in their direction' which they imagined was 'our own Native Contingent'. It was, regretfully, to prove a misinterpretation. Soon afterwards, the first hint of danger materialised as three or four horsemen on the Natal side of the river furiously galloped in the direction of the Rorke's Drift post. Again Reynolds innocently believed that they might be messengers calling for additional medical assistance to the distant battle and hurried down to his hospital. As they neared the post, however, Reynolds' heart must have missed a beat as he observed 'the awfully scared' expression on their faces and the fact that one of them was riding a pony which he recognised belonged to his colleague, Surgeon Major Shepherd (earlier assegaied in the frantic retreat from Isandlwana). The terrible truth soon dawned as they shouted, 'the camp at Isandlwana has been taken by the enemy' and 'all our men in it massacred and that no power could stand against the enormous number of Zulus and the only chance for us all was by immediate flight'. (AMCM Reynolds Report)

A few hundred yards away, at around 3.15pm, Chard was himself greeted by identical news from two other panic-stricken European riders. This time, Chard guessed 'from their

# Lieutenant Gonville 'Gonny' Bromhead VC (1845–1891)

## Second-in-Command, Battle of Rorke's Drift

Bromhead was born into a distinguished military family in Versailles, France, on 29 August 1845. His father, Edmund de Gonville Bromhead, fought and lost an eye as a 54th Regiment lieutenant at Waterloo. His uncle commanded the 77th Regiment at El Bodon and his grandfather served in the American War of Independence and was captured at Saratoga. His great-grandfather served with Wolfe at Quebec in 1759. His eldest brother fought in the Crimea, another brother was killed in the Second Afghan War and his youngest brother also served in the 24th Regiment in the Ashanti Campaign.

Bromhead was educated at Thomas Magnus School in Newark-on-Trent where, at 1.78m tall and stockily built, he became a champion at boxing, wrestling and singlestick. He joined the 24th Foot as an ensign by purchase on 20 April 1867 and was commissioned as a lieutenant in 1871. Whilst confident in the regimental mess he could be awkward with strangers. This may have been due to a serious hearing problem and might also account for the views of some senior officers that he was dull and inactive.

On 28 January 1878 Bromhead's 2nd Battalion was called up for active service in the Cape and his B Company was involved in a number of actions around King Williams Town in the closing stages of the Cape Frontier War. Transferred to Durban his company joined No. 3 Column. On 9 January 1879, just before the expiry of Frere's ultimatum, Bromhead and his B Company arrived at Rorke's Drift and, after Chelmsford's main column crossed the Buffalo River on 11 January, was left behind to garrison the depot.

On 22 January, Bromhead received the terrible news of the attack at Isandlwana and he was to play a pivotal role in the defence of Rorke's Drift.

His post-war career was sadly short-lived. After service in Burma and the East Indies and promotion to major in 1883, he was struck down by enteric or typhoid fever at Allahabad Barracks, India, 9 February 1891. (Sources: Greaves and Knight, *Who's Who in the Zulu War*, Vol. 1, p.35; Bancroft, *Zulu War VCs*, p.35)

*Lieutenant Gonville Bromhead VC, the second-in-command at Rorke's Drift. (JY)*

gesticulations and shouts' that 'something was the matter'. After ferrying the men across the river, one of them, Lieutenant Adendorff of Lonsdale's Regiment, the Natal Native Contingent – later to play an enigmatic role in the siege – promptly jumped off his horse, took Chard to one side and told him that the camp was in the hands of the Zulu and the army destroyed. Lord Chelmsford and the rest of the column, he added, had probably shared the same fate. Chard, noting his high excitement and demonstrating coolness and presence of mind, even at this terrifying juncture, expressed some doubt and intimated that he probably had not remained to see what did occur.

Chard's initial incredulity on receiving this horrifying news was shared by another of his men, Private Waters. He greeted the frantic massage of another desperate survivor, Private Evans, arriving terribly dishevelled 'without coat or cap on' 'with profound disbelief'. Private Henry Hook, positioned alongside Lieutenant Bromhead in the camp area, met the same horseman but, unlike Waters, was mortified by news of his dear comrades 'butchered to a man'. He anxiously watched as Bromhead also received the fateful official confirmation note from Captain Alan Gardner of No. 3 Column, informing him that, 'the enemy was coming on and that the post was to be held at all costs'. It was the first test of the garrison 'morale but they passed it with flying colours'. Hook significantly recalled how, 'for some we were all stunned then everything changed from perfect quietness to intense excitement and energy'. (Accounts taken from, Holme, *Silver Wreath*, Waters and Hook Accounts, pp.59, 63)

## Preparations for Defence

There was certainly no lack of energy amongst the officers. Chard's conversation with Adendorff at the river was soon interrupted by the receipt of an urgent message from Lieutenant Bromhead requesting him to return 'at once' to his post at the Commissariat stores. Before departing, Chard gave an order to load and to inspan (harness) the wagon. He then posted his NCO and six men to a stronger position on high ground above the pont, perched on a natural wall of rocks and with a far better view of the river and tactical ground beyond it. He left orders for them to wait until he returned or until he sent for them. Galloping up to the Commissariat stores, he was handed the pencilled warning note from Isandlwana survivor Captain Alan Gardner, confirming that the enemy were advancing on Rorke's Drift in force. Bromhead accordingly sent an urgent message forward to Helpmekaar via two mounted infantrymen, also refugees from Isandlwana, detailing the news of the dire situation now confronting the garrison and the whole region.

Soon two key assistants, Acting Assistant Commissary James Dalton and Surgeon Major Reynolds, joined Chard and Bromhead to discuss the options for survival against what was clearly going to be an overwhelmingly superior Zulu strike force. With this in mind, Bromhead had already, on his own initiative, given orders to strike the camp and had even loaded up the two garrison wagons ready for departure. It was at this point that Dalton made a crucial tactical intervention, which, in hindsight, probably saved the garrison. Private Hook recalled:

> Mr Dalton of the Commissariat Department came up and said that if we left the Drift every man was certain to be killed. It was excellent advice. Chased by up to 4000 highly mobile Zulu warriors, such a slow-moving convoy of men and wagons, heavily encumbered by over 30 sick patients, would have been easily tracked, rapidly overtaken and destroyed in open country.
> Holme, *Silver Wreath*, Hook Account, p.63

In Reynolds' words, 'removing the sick and wounded would have been embarrassing to our movement and desertion of them was never thought of.' (AMCM, Reynolds Report)

Having wisely accepted Dalton's advice, Chard and Bromhead conducted a 'short and earnest' conversation, both officers clearly remembering and deeply appreciating Dalton's 'energy,

The Battlefield: What Actually Happened?

*Modern view across the front perimeter of Rorke's Drift, stones now marking the approximate line of the mealie-bag wall. (EY)*

intelligence and gallantry – a man of the greatest service to us.' (Holme, *Silver Wreath*, Chard Account, p.50)

All three officers then toured the garrison area. Later, as Chard hurriedly left to close down the Pont operations on the river, Bromhead, Dalton and the ever-supportive Surgeon Reynolds, supervised the barricading and loop-holing of the store building and hospital, connecting the two buildings by a defensive wall of mealie bags and the two wagons which were hurriedly emptied and upturned. As Private Hook observed, these heavy-duty stores proved to be a godsend for the construction of the walls:

> The mealie bags were good, big heavy things weighing about two hundred pounds each... the biscuit boxes contained ordinary biscuit. The were big, square, wooden boxes weighing about a hundred weight each. The meat boxes, too, were very heavy as they contained tinned meat. They were smaller than the biscuit boxes. Even barrels of rum and lime juice were pressed into service.
>
> Holme, *Silver Wreath*, Hook Account, p.63

*Mr W.A. Dunne,*
*Commissariat Department.*
*(JY)*

MR. W. A. DUNNE, COMMISSARIAT DEPARTMENT
One of the Defenders of Rorke's Drift

On his return to the river, Chard experienced an incident which provided a remarkable foretaste of the incredible courage, resilience and fighting spirit now emerging from within this small group of British soldiers. With the ponts floated in mid-stream and both the hausers and cables duly sunk, the ferryman, Mr Daniels, and Sergeant Milne, 3rd Buffs, spontaneously offered to defend the ponts from their position in the middle of the river while Sergeant Williams and his small 24th Guard contingent also indicated their willingness to join them. This risky, but nonetheless courageous gesture, undoubtedly provided a massive boost to Chard's morale, acutely conscious as he was of the enormity of the threat confronting his diminutive force.

Back at the Rorke's Drift post, Bromhead, assisted by Dalton and all the available able-bodied men, had frantically continued completing the barricades. Colour Sergeant Bourne particularly recalled the usefulness of the two Boer transport wagons which comprised 'excellent barricades' as part of the back wall connecting the front of the Commissariat with the rear of the

# The Battlefield: What Actually Happened?

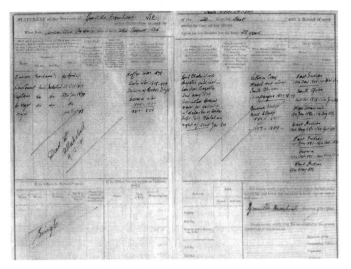

*Lieutenant Bromhead's service record. (PB)*

hospital, 'During these early stages at least the several 100-strong Natal Native Contingent, commanded by Captain Stevenson, proved vital support in the frenzied process of extending and reinforcing the Rorke's Drift defences'. Dunne confirmed their initially important role: 'It was well for us that we had help of the three hundred natives at this juncture, otherwise the works would not have been accomplished in time.'

Lieutenant Bromhead was also proving his worth as a competent line officer by setting up vedette and watch positions. Private Hitch was accordingly despatched to the top of the storehouse to report any signs of the approaching Zulu force. Responsibility for this essential work was also delegated to the NCOs with, for instance, Sergeant Bourne, detailed to organise men stationed in the hospital as lookouts, post others to designated vulnerable points and to deploy a line of skirmishers.

In fact the NCOs were fast proving to be the backbone of the garrison. Sergeant Windridge was a case in point and his reliability and steadfastness were key in sustaining morale. He was specifically tasked with securing the casks of rum, with additional orders to shoot anyone who attempted to force his post, and he further demonstrated, 'great intelligence and energy' by 'arranging the store… forming loop-holes etc'. (Holme, *Silver Wreath*, Chard Account, p.50)

For Surgeon Major Reynolds, it was the ingenuity, efficiency and energy of Dalton and Chard which had proved 'invaluable'. Dalton, he recalled:

> without the smallest delay, which would have been so fatal for us… called upon the men (all eager for doing) to carry the mealie sacks here and there for defences, and it was charming to find in a short time how comparatively protected we had made ourselves.
>
> AMCM, Reynolds Report

Chard, he also remembered:

> arriving as the work was in progress, gave many practical orders as regards the line of defence. His practical engineering mind was everywhere in evidence amongst the veritable whirl of activity, during which even the walking sick were commandeered from the hospital and utilised for the lighter tasks.
>
> [Chard] approved also of the Hospital being taken in and, between the Hospital orderlies, convalescent patients (eight or ten) and myself, we loop-holed the building and made a continuation of the Commissariat defences around it…
>
> AMCM, Reynolds Report

In purely morale terms, Dalton was commonly perceived as the main symbol of defiance, 'as brave a soldier as ever lived', who when:

> hearing the terrible news said now we must make a defence! It was his suggestion which decided us to form a breast work of

bags of grain, boxes of biscuits and everything that would help stop a bullet or keep out a man.

AMCM, Dunne, *Waggoner*, Reminiscences

Other vital preparations included the filling of the station water barrel which was brought inside the outer perimeter, and perhaps, most crucially (bearing in mind the earlier still much-debated logistical/supply difficulties at Isandlwana), the opening of several boxes of ammunition which were judiciously placed at several strategic points. All together up to 20,000 Martini-Henry rounds were available for the forthcoming battle. All these endeavours soon bore fruit and, astonishingly, within two hours, a nearly complete wall, around 4ft high, had been constructed around the post. It was a wall which incorporated both the hospital and store buildings.

Amidst all these intense defensive preparations there was at least one amusing episode. On returning from an early afternoon ride, a heartbroken, unsuspecting Reverend Witt had been traumatised when he witnessed the severe damage caused to his beloved mission buildings. Nevertheless, as Trooper Harry Lugg recalled, his over-dramatic protests became the subject of great mirth for the already tense, dust-covered and sweating soldiers:

No-one could help laughing at their gesticulations when they came back on seeing their best parlour paper being pulled down and loop-holes being knocked out, while splendid furniture was scattered about. His first question was, in broken English, ''vot is dish?'. Someone replied that the Zulus were almost upon us, upon which he bolted, saying, 'Mein Gott, mein wife and mein children at Umsinga! Oh mein Gott!'

Emery, *Red Soldier*, p.132

There were some far more unwelcome interruptions. A succession of doom-laden Isandlwana survivors continued to arrive at the post, much to the chagrin of the NCOs and particularly Lieutenant Chard, who were all understandably concerned at the potentially disastrous impact upon garrison morale. One fugitive accordingly whispered to the twenty-four-year-old, surprisingly youthful but otherwise immutable, Colour Sergeant Bourne, 'not a fighting chance for you young fellow'. Other survivors insensitively informed an already nervous Private Hook that the Zulus would be 'up in two or three minutes'. Likewise, a mounted infantryman and two of his 'excited and breathless' fellow Natal Mounted Police, Troopers Shannon and Doig, approached Trooper Lugg who recalled, upon my asking, 'what is it, is it true?' Doig replied, 'You will all be murdered' and he rode off with his comrade'. Fortunately Lugg, 'steadied his nerves', bravely asserting that 'Nothing remains but to fight and that we will do to the bitter end'. (Holme, *Silver Wreath*, Bourne Account, p.50; Emery, *Red Soldier*, p.126 and Lugg Account, p.132)

Chard remained singularly unimpressed, indeed contemptuous of such men, most of whom refused to stay and help, as well as being angered by the constant distractions they caused to the vital work of reinforcing the defences. He later wrote:

> Who they were I do not know but it is scarcely necessary for me to say that there were no officers of Her Majesty's Army among them. They stopped the work very much – it being impossible to prevent the men getting round them in little groups to hear their story. They proved the truth of their belief in what they said by leaving us to our fate, and in the state of mind they were in. I think our little garrison was as well without them.
>
> Holme, *Silver Wreath*, Chard Account, p.50

In fact, in the face of all these pressures the morale of the garrison remained amazingly high, responding heartily to one officer's rallying cry that 'we were never to say die or surrender'.

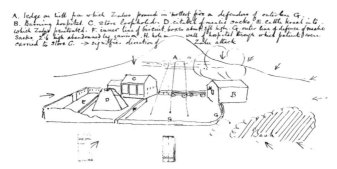

*A rare contemporary sketch of the siege of Rorke's Drift, clearly showing the direction of the Zulu assaults and the organisation of the defences. Author unknown. (RRWM)*

## A Defensive Assessment

It is, perhaps, useful at this point to assess the soundness of Rorke's Drift as a defensive position. In retrospect, Captain Hallam Parr considered it intrinsically weak, a comment which in itself might be considered a backhanded compliment to the subsequent bravery and resourcefulness of the defenders:

> A worse position could hardly be imagined. Two small thatched buildings about 39 yards apart with their walls commanded by rising ground on the south and west, completely overlooked on the south by a high hill. On the north side an orchard and garden gave access to an enemy up to within a few yards of the houses.

> Hallam Parr, *Sketch*, p.237

Several of the defenders were conscious of such weaknesses. Surgeon Reynolds observed that, at first sight,

> … the Hospital, for instance, occupied a wretched position having a garden and shrubbery close by which often proved

so favourable to the enemy [but] compared with that of the Isandhlwana affair we felt that the mealie barriers might afford us a moderately fair chance.

AMCM, Reynolds Report

Dunne was also very concerned by another glaring shortcoming in the hospital defences. Touring the area just before the battle commenced, he spotted an extremely vulnerable section of the back wall which, in his view, was the:

… weakest point, for there was nothing but a plank to close the opening at one part; but before anything could be done to strengthen it a shot was fired outside – the Zulu had arrived.

AMCM, Dunne, *Waggoner*, Reminiscences

While it was true that the two thatched buildings were a major disadvantage, prone to being fired on (as one subsequently was), they were, as mentioned, in fact only about 30 yards apart, making it relatively easy to construct a defensive wall between them. In front of them was a patch of flat ground which dropped away in a rocky ledge to 4ft high. With the mealie bag wall placed firmly on top of that ledge reaching around 7ft or 8ft in height, the front of the post did provide a formidable obstacle for a Zulu enemy primarily armed with shields, assegais and knobkerries, notwithstanding the cover provided by the orchard and shrubbery. Moreover, the buildings, particularly to the rear, had very few doors and windows, and with loop-holes knocked through them, provided a good potential protection for defenders deployed at these positions. Overall, around the Mission, there was little room for the Zulus to manoeuvre *en masse*. The ground in front, with trees and shrubs, was awkward in terms of enemy cover, but in essence there was effectively a killing zone all round the buildings within 30 or 40 yards. Nevertheless, the close proximity of the Oskarsberg Hill directly overlooking the garrison was, as all contemporary observers confirmed, a major tactical problem, and many of the garrison's casualties were to be caused by Zulu sniper fire from this dominating position.

At around 3.30pm, an officer of Durnford's ill-fated Natal Native Horse arrived, accompanied by several score of nervous riders. It appeared to be a welcome reinforcement and a delighted Chard duly requested him to, firstly, observe enemy movements and, secondly, check the Zulu advance as much as possible until they were forced to fall back. Events now moved rapidly. Although much of the defensive works were completed, there remained some worrying gaps principally around the dog leg barrier in front of the hospital. Reynolds at least felt relieved to find that his two colleagues, the Reverend Otto Witt and Chaplain Smith had returned safely from the hill where they had been mistakenly convinced, 'up to a late moment' that the approaching Zulu force were 'our own men'. The two reported that the *impi*, led by two mounted men (one of whom was certainly the Zulu commander, Dabulamanzi), had crossed the river by a drift about a mile away in typical arms – linked Zulu fashion – in a tactical manoeuvre which suggested a possible attack on the rear of the Rorke's Drift post. They had watched as the Zulus had crossed in three bodies and, after snuff-taking and other ceremonies, had recommenced their advance. (AMCM, Reynolds Report)

At around 4.20pm, the:

> … sound of firing was heard from behind the Oscarberg. The battle for Rorke's Drift had begun. As the outposts sprinted in there was barely time for the last non-combatants to escape. The Reverend Witt now took this last opportunity to ride away to try to secure the safety of his family stranded on a local farm at Umsinga. By stark contrast army chaplain, the Reverend George Smith, was left trapped… as his Kaffir groom had bolted and apparently taken with him his horse.
>
> AMCM, Reynolds Report

## Desertion and Defensive Redeployment

Chard remained relatively confident, having more than enough fighting power (over 300 white-officered NNC, NNH and white regulars), to man the almost complete defensive perimeter. At this critical juncture, however, as the first Zulu skirmishers tentatively appeared two potentially catastrophic events occurred, either of which could have fatally undermined garrison morale and cohesion.

The first blow was delivered when the 100-odd mounted NNH survivors of Durnford's force suddenly returned from their vedette positions – not, alas, to stay and fight, but to retreat to the next British post at Helpmekaar. Their commanding officer merely stopped to report that the enemy were 'close upon us and that his men will not obey his orders'. It must have been a bitter blow especially as the Zulu were known to have 'a mortal terror of cavalry', and this sizeable force might have deterred their Zulu attackers or played a key role in driving back or even dispersing them.

Worse was to follow. 'At about the same time', having already absorbed news of the horrors of Isandlwana, heard the first shots signalling an imminent Zulu attack, the whole of the 100–300 strong NNC 'took up their assegais' and, with their white officers, promptly bolted.

In a flash a garrison of up to 400 fighting effectives, was reduced to barely 100. Nevertheless, this potentially unnerving spectacle, rather than instigating mass panic, produced a variety of robust responses, ranging from anger to relief or just simply pragmatism. Some soldiers of the 2/24th, notably Private Hook, were even enraged for, 'to see them deserting like that was too much for some of us and we fired after them'. (Holme, *Silver Wreath*, Hook Account, p.63) The sergeant was struck and killed (other sources note that this was probably a corporal, Corporal W. Anderson). While there is only one specific mention of an African member of the NNC being hit it is highly likely that more were wounded, if not killed. By contrast Sergeant Bourne, demonstrating maturity beyond his twenty-three years, remained calm and philosophical. Having later claimed, with grim satisfaction, that the European NNC officers were arrested some days later, tried and dismissed from the service, he concluded:

> The desertion of this detachment of 200 men appeared, at first sight, to be a special loss with only a hundred or so of us left, but the feeling afterwards was that we could not have trusted them, and, also, that our defence was too small to accommodate them anyhow.
>
> Holme, *Silver Wreath*, Bourne Account, p.60

Chard, although undoubtedly shocked by the suddenness of this departure and annoyed that the officer had 'deserted us', was more pragmatic. Immediately recognising the need to consolidate the now undermined and overextended defences, he commenced a retrenchment of biscuit boxes, 'so as to get a place where we could fall back upon if we could not hold the whole'. Private Hook recalled with admiration this clever tactical ploy:

> As soon as the Kaffirs bolted, it was seen that the fort as we had first made it was too large to be held so Lieutenant Chard instantly reduced the space by bringing a row of biscuit boxes down across the middle about four feet high. This was our inner retrenchment and proved very valuable.
>
> Holme, *Silver Wreath*, Hook Account, p.63

In an interview recorded just before the twenty-fifth anniversary of the battle, Surgeon Reynolds praised this tactic, but mistakenly gave the credit for it to Lieutenant Bromhead:

> Bromhead at this point, certainly saved the situation by cutting the laager in half by means of biscuit tins. But for that we should have been smashed to pieces – not a doubt of it. He saw

*The Zulu perspective of the view of Rorke's Drift as they commenced their first assault. (EY)*

the wisdom of concentrating our defence in the nick of time, and accomplished it.

AMCM, Reynolds Report

## Initial sightings (4.20–4.30pm approximately)

Here and there a black body doubled up, and went writhing and bouncing into the dust; but the great host came steadily on, spreading out – spreading out – spreading out till they seemed like a giant pair of nutcrackers opening around the little nut of Rorke's Drift. It was nasty, really nasty, the inevitability of that silent (mass) closing in upon us.

AMCM, Surgeon Reynolds, 'How VCs are Won'

In fact, it was only a few minutes before the shrunken garrison encountered the first Zulu assault. Private Hitch, from his elevated vantage point on top of the house, first observed the ominous approach of forward elements of the 4,000-strong *impi*. As soon as he reached the top, he could see the advancing Zulus were already at the other side of the rise and extending for attack. The following brief, almost flippant, conversation with Lieutenant Bromhead occurred as the news was conveyed by Hitch to him and the men in the yard below:

> I told Mr Bromhead… they were extending for the attack, Mr Bromhead asked me 'how many they were?' I told him I thought (they) numbered up to 4–6000. A voice from below – 'is that all, we can manage that lot very well for a few seconds!!'
>
> Holme, *Silver Wreath*, Hitch Account, p.62

Such apparent frivolity belied the huge tension within the garrison, as outnumbered by as much as thirty to one, they prepared for a desperate struggle for survival.

Surgeon Reynolds recalled being mesmerised by the awesome initial sighting of the enemy, as:

> … a swarm of Zulus came round the crook of the mountain at a slow, slinging trot, spreading themselves out in skirmishing order and made straight at us, an innumerable swarm of blacks. They came in perfect silence – no war whoops, no dancing, no shouting, and holding their fire. Striking-looking figures of great physical beauty, the Martini in one hand the assegai slung across the back – fresh from the massacre of Isandlana, running in perfect silence to wipe out the little body of left behinds at Rorkes Drift.
>
> AMCM, Reynolds interview, 'How VCs are won'

Assistant Commissary Walter Dunne also remembered the eerie silence of the first Zulu approach, a 'black mass coming on without a sound at a steady trot', while Sergeant Bourne observed them 'driving in my thin red line of skirmishers' to make 'a rush at our south wall'. Corporal Lyons was also struck by the silence of the approach. 'The Zulus did not shout, as they generally do, but, after extending and forming a half moon they steadily advanced and kept up a tremendous fire'. Private Waters was more impressed by their discipline – fifty of them 'forming a line in skirmishing order, just as British soldiers would do'. (Dunne, *Waggoner*; Holme, *Silver Wreath*, Bourne Account, p.60 and Lyons and Waters Accounts, pp.59 and 61)

## Opening Shots

Private Hitch probably represented the first identifiable target for the approaching Zulu lead elements, as he watched them deploying in front of the Oskarsberg and creeping under the rocks with snipers taking cover in the caves. A number of shots were in fact fired at him, but fortunately for him, 'their direction was good

*The caves where Zulu snipers were posted on the Oskarsberg Hill. (EY)*

## ZULU WEAPONRY

Zulu weaponry was basic but deadly in terms of close-quarter fighting. By Cetshwayo's time, each warrior still carried the short, extremely sharp, broad-bladed stabbing spear (*ikilwa*), ostensibly introduced by Shaka. In more recent years, this standard weapon had been supplemented by a number of throwing spears (*izijula*).

but their elevation bad'. Hitch 'fired three shots these being the first that were fired at the Zulus at Rorke's Drift'. (Holme, *Silver Wreath*, p.62; also Emery, *Red Soldier*, p.136)

So far, aside from the folly of attacking a defended post, the initial tactics of Dabulamanzai and his *indunas* were relatively sound. He was already testing the weakest line of defence around the hospital, and the posting of snipers on top of the Oskarsberg Hill gave him some valuable intelligence regarding the numbers and deployment of the garrison as well as a clearly defined killing ground. Hitch spotted the problem immediately with a sole Zulu vedette, 'On the top of the mountain; from the other side he could see us in the laager plain enough to count us'. Private Hitch then tried to pick him off but 'my shot fell short of him'. (Holme, *Silver Wreath*, p.62)

The opening shots from the rest of the garrison were, according to Dunne, fired at the relatively extreme range of 800 yards, not the most accurate distance for the Martini-Henry rifle. Dunne noted, however, that the men on the south wall: 'Dropped many of the foremost causing the remainder to swerve away to their left and thus move to the front of our position.' (Dunne, *Waggoner*)

Private Hitch meanwhile kept up a running commentary to Lieutenant Bromhead, noting the increasing concentration of Zulu warriors in the caves and informing Bromhead that they would be 'all around us in a very short time'. Chaplain Smith also nervously watched as the Zulus took rapid possession of the 'rocks overlooking our buildings and the barricades at the back with the caves and crevices quickly filled – from these the enemy poured down a continuous fire upon us'. (Holme, *Silver Wreath*, Hitch Account, p.62; and Lummis, *Smith Diary*, p.52)

At 500–600 yards range, the advancing first wave of the 600-strong Zulu iNdluyengwe Regiment experienced their first serious casualties. Surgeon Reynolds was somewhat frustrated by the continuing ineffectiveness of these opening volleys, as the Zulu 'seemed quite regardless of the danger'. What again struck Reynolds and many other members of the garrison as 'most strange' was that 'not only was there no war-cry but nor did they at this time fire a single shot in return'. The British rifle fire was initially 'a little wild'. This was undoubtedly due to battle nerves, the common problem of establishing range, and possibly some hesitation, as according to Lyons, the men were told 'not to fire without orders… this… was to make sure that the advancing force was really Zulus'. It was an extremely tense beginning, Reynolds reaffirming that 'we were little put to it by the impotence of our volley'. (AMCM, Reynolds Report; Holme, *Silver Wreath*, Lyons Account, p.61)

Zulu casualties quickly mounted, however, as a few yards further on they were met by a much more 'steady and deliberate fire'. Gunner Howard, stationed in the hospital and borrowing sick Sergeant Maxfield's Martini-Henry rifle, commenced opening fire at 400 yards. His initial battle nerves were very evident:

> When I beheld the swarm I said to myself, 'all up now', but I was wrong and we all agreed to fight until two were left and these were to shoot themselves. Great execution was done as when the Zulus were about 400 yards off, like a wall coming on, we fired the first volley. The rifles being Martini-Henrys our firing was very quick, and, when struck by the bullets, the niggers [sic] would give a spring in the air and fall flat down. The enemy advance to within 300 yards and then it did not seem healthy to come any nearer…

> Emery, *Red Soldier*, p.134

A similarly tense Trooper Harry Lugg 'told off in my turn' to take a loop-hole and saddled with a broken Martini-Henry carbine, the stock 'bent' and tied up with a rein, opened fire at around 350 yards and he:

> had the satisfaction of seeing the first I fired at roll over… and then my nerves were as steady as a rock. I made sure, almost before I pulled the trigger. There was some of the best shooting at 450 yards I have ever seen.

Emery, *Red Soldier*, p.132

Demonstrating great initiative, Corporals Lyons and Allen as well as Private Dunbar played a key role in breaking up the impetus of the first Zulu assault. Lyons, Allen and several other men formed a cohesive unit to 'check the fire from the enemy's right flank as it was thought the crack shots would go up there. We all consider we did good service.' Alongside these men was the stirring sight of their indefatigable officer Lieutenant Bromhead 'on the right face, firing over the mealies with a Martini-Henry'. Private Dunbar excelled himself, and in several accounts emerges as the real hero of this opening phase of the battle. A crack shot, he scored several hits at 500–600 yards including 'a chief on horseback'. The early loss of a leading Zulu commander probably came as a distinct shock to many of the Zulu attackers. One can only speculate on the major

*Corporal William Allen VC (RRWM)*

71

impact on Zulu morale if the other horseman, almost certainly the senior commander Dabulamanzi, had been the victim. Private Hook later claimed that Dunbar 'shot no fewer than nine Zulus… one of them being a chief'. Chaplain Smith gave Dunbar a slightly smaller tally, 'eight Zulus, killed with consecutive shots as they came round the ledge of the hill'. (Holme, *Silver Wreath*, Lyons, Chard and Hook Accounts, pp.51, 61, 64; Lummis, *Smith Diary*, p.52)

This first Zulu onslaught was not as wild or reckless as some contemporary commentators have suggested. Several of the garrison remembered the prolonged disciplined and methodical pattern of the traditional Zulu attack with snipers providing covering fire. Private Hitch remembered: 'they attacked us in the shape of a bullocks horn and in a few minutes were all around us.' Harry Lugg also marvelled at the cohesiveness of their formation, as the Zulu 'came on first in sections of four then opened out skirmishing order and up came their reserve and then they were on us'. All were impressed by the excellent use of the terrain by the advancing Zulu. (Holme, *Silver Wreath*, Hitch Account, p.6; Emery, *Red Soldier*, Lugg Account, p.132)

Hook recalled how:

> During the fight they took advantage of every bit of cover there was; ant hills, a tract of bush, that we had not time to clear away, a garden or sort of orchard which was near and a ledge of rock and some caves (on the Oskarsberg) which were only about 100 yards away. They neglected nothing…!
>
> Holme, *Silver Wreath*, Hook Account, p.63

Surgeon Reynolds cursed the tactical disadvantages of the garden and shrubbery which the Zulus skilfully used to:

> Pour in upon us a galling fire. It was a frightful oversight – the leaving of that garden and shrubbery. Heavens! They rained lead on us at the distance of a cricket pitch or two.
>
> AMCM, Reynolds, 'How VCs are Won'

*This front view of Rorke's Drift demonstrates how effectively the Zulu snipers based on the Oskarsberg to the rear could dominate the garrison, especially the front wall defenders. (AB)*

In fact, the garrison had little or no time to clear the area before the Zulu arrival – the main focus necessarily being on strengthening the core inner defences. As Chard later reported:

> the bush grew close to our wall and we had not time to cut it down. The enemy were thus able to advance under cover close to our wall, and in this part soon held one side of the wall while we held the other.
>
> Holme, *Silver Wreath*, Chard Account, p.51

At 50 yards, the first Zulu wave were truly decimated by all out volley fire from the defenders which forced them to divert to the left and complete the encirclement of the garrison as well as probe for any weakness in the perimeter. The men in the loop-holed store were accordingly able 'to do great execution at that side', whilst 'semi-flank fire from another part of the laager played on them destructively'. Also, the 'loop-holes in the hospital were made great use of so that the combined fire had the effect of keeping the Zulus at bay'. Harry Lugg recalled the terrible impact of this enfilading fire on the first Zulu echelon who comprised the relatively young inDluyengwe Regiment: 'They were caught between two fires, that from the hospital and that from the storehouse and were checked.' Nevertheless, the Zulu used cover well, 'gaining the shelter of the cookhouse and delivering many heavy volleys'. Both Corporal Francis Attwood and Lieutenant Adendorff played a crucial role here, Attwood firing from an upper window in the storehouse wall and Adendorff from another loop-hole 'flanking the wall and Hospital – his rifle did good service'. (AMCM, Reynolds Report; Emery, *Red Soldier*, Lugg Account, p.132; Holme, *Silver Wreath*, Chard and Hook Accounts, pp.50, 127)

## Phase 2: Assegai against Bayonet

The main battle commences at the barricades.

| 22 January 1879 | c.4.45pm | Main Zulu regiments arrive and deploy into the bush in front of the post. Zulu snipers occupy the caves and rocks of the Shiyane terraces and open fire |
| | c.5pm | The battle intensifies and focuses on the hospital porch area, a notable incomplete weak point in the hospital defences. British casualties mount due to Zulu sniper fire from the Shiyane heights. Bromhead organises bayonet parties to reinforce vulnerable points |

## The Battlefield: What Actually Happened?

It was a soldiers battle – each man fighting for his own hand.
RLCM, Assistant Commissary Dunne, *Waggoner*

Along most sections of the outside perimeter, both sides were now pitched eyeball to eyeball and the nerves of the British soldiers and their Zulu protagonists were to be tested to the utmost. Until then, the British deploying their devastating volley fire, clearly had technical superiority, but with close-quarter fighting at the barricades in which assegais, knobkerries, rifle butts and bayonets were the dominant weaponry, the two sides were more equally matched. Over the next hour or so:

> reinforced by some hundreds they made desperate and repeated attempts to break through our temporary defences, but were repulsed time and again. To show their fearlessness and their contempt for the red coats and small numbers, they tried to leap the parapet, and, at times, seized our bayonets, only to be shot down. Looking back, one cannot but admire their fanatical bravery.
> Holme, *Silver Wreath*, Bourne Account, p.60

Individual British soldiers demonstrated extraordinary coolness and courage. Hitch, realising that the Zulus were now too close for rifle fire, slid down the thatch and dropped down into the laager area taking his position in an uncompleted open space, 'as the deadly work now commenced'. At this second stage of the battle, the bravery of three particular garrison members on the barricades stood out – Dalton, Byrne and Scheiss. 'Dalton fearlessly exposing himself… cheering the men and using his own rifle most effectively.' When one Zulu ran up near the barricade, Mr Dalton called out 'pot that fellow' and himself aimed over the parapet at another. (Holme, *Silver Wreath*, Hitch Account, p.62; Lummis, *Smith Diary*, p.52)

The sheer voracity of the Zulu attacks in this period belied their alleged fatigue. The north-west line of mealie bags beside the hospital came under the most sustained pressure. Here Dalton shot a Zulu who was in the act of assegaing a corporal of the

Army Hospital Corps, the muzzle of whose rifle he had seized. Chard testified to the relentless pressure exerted on this section of the garrison by the endless waves of Zulu warriors:

> A series of desperate assaults was made on the hospital and extending from the hospital as far as the bush reached; but each was most splendidly met and repulsed by our men, with the bayonet. Each time as the attack was repulsed by us, the Zulus close to us seemed to vanish in the bush, those some little distance off keeping up a fire all the time. Then, as if moved by a single impulse, they rose in the bush as thick as possible, rushing madly up to the wall (some of them being already close to it), seizing, where they could, the muzzles of our men's rifles or their bayonets, attempting to use their assegais and to get over the wall. A rapid rattle of fire from our rifles, stabs with the bayonets, and in a few moments the Zulus were driven back, disappearing in the bush as before, and keeping up their fire. A brief interval, and the attack would be again made, and repulsed in the same manner. Over and over again this happened, our men behaving with the greatest coolness and gallantry.
>
> Holme, *Silver Wreath*, Chard Account, p.51

*A close-up view of the Shiyane or Oskarsberg terraces behind Rorke's Drift which provided such excellent cover for the Zulu snipers. (EY)*

## The Battlefield: What Actually Happened?

For a while, the battle stabilised in these static positions, but the garrison was already taking unnecessarily high casualties, not at the barricades but from the Zulu snipers stationed high up on the Oskarsberg or Shiyane terraces. Although clearly unfamiliar with the very few Martini-Henry rifles which they had already looted from fugitives from the Isandlwana battle, the effect of concentrated fire of these and their other obsolete firearms, in such a small area was bound to result in serious injuries or death. Determined to 'check' the flank firing as much as possible, Corporal Lyons with his neighbour Corporal Allen, found a good counter-sniper position:

> … we fired many shots and I said to my comrade 'They, the Zulus are falling fast over there' and he replied 'yes we are giving it to them'. I saw many Zulus killed on the hill.
>
> Holme, *Silver Wreath*, Lyons Account, p.61

Smith in his diary (Lummis, p.53) in particular noted the deadly effect of Zulu snipers on the exposed front wall position with five men 'shot dead in a very short space of time'. Such losses were to represent nearly one-third of the garrison's final death toll. Chard was acutely aware of his men's vulnerability from this particular threat at this stage of the battle:

> The fire from the rocks and caves on the hills behind us was kept up all the time and took us completely in reverse… although very badly directed many shots came amongst us and caused us some loss.
>
> Holme, *Silver Wreath*, Chard Account, p.51

Thus Private Fred Hitch:

> saw one of my comrades – Private Nichols – killed; he was shot through the head, his brains being scattered all about us… He had, up to his death, been doing good service with his rifle.
>
> Emery, *Red Soldier*, pp.136–7

*The side and rear of the rebuilt garrison hospital today. The front porch was heavily assaulted by Zulu attackers. (AB)*

Under such intense pressure, some sections of the 'thin red line' began to waver and the first Zulu were able to penetrate and pressurise the weakest point in the British defences, the hospital porch. A ferocious struggle took place around there, during which one British weapon, the 'lunger' bayonet, had an unexpected shock impact on the Zulu attackers. Hitch provided the main account of this critical juncture in the battle:

> The Zulus pushing right up to the porch, it was not until the bayonet was freely used that they flinched at least a bit. Had the Zulus taken the bayonet as freely as they took the bullets, we could not have stood more than fifteen minutes. They pushed right up to us and not only got up to the laager but got in with us, but they seemed to have a great dread of the bayonet, which stood us from beginning to end.
>
> Holme, *Silver Wreath*, Hitch Account, p.62

Why this should be so is a mystery, but it is quite possible that some Zulu were unnerved by their inexperience with this weapon. The Undi Corps were historically unfamiliar with this weapon which was not used by their more familiar Boer enemy. Furthermore, the shorter stabbing spear may have proved less flexible or effective when pitched against the deeper and considerably longer thrusts of the combined Martini-Henry rifle and bayonet. Zulu frustration as to how to deal with this British weapon may also have been reflected in the several Brtish eyewitness accounts of their often futile attempts to wrench the bayonets from the muzzles of soldiers rifles. Chaplain Smith recalled at least two instances when intrepid Zulu warriors, 'succeeded in wrestling them off the rifles, but the two bold perpetrators were instantly shot'. (Lummis, *Smith Diary*, p.52)

It was indeed a life and death struggle in the most brutal sense. Private Hitch provided yet another rare vignette of the sustained intensity and ferocity of the hand-to-hand combat within the porch area:

> During that struggle there was a fine big Zulu see me shoot his mate down – he sprang forward, dropping his rifle and assegais and seizing hold of the muzzle of my rifle with his left hand and the right hand hold of the bayonet. Thinking to disarm me, he pulled and tried hard to get the rifle from me, but I had a firm hold of the small of the butt of my rifle with my left hand. My cartridges on the top of the mealie bags… enabled me to load my rifle and (I) shot the poor wretch whilst holding on to his grasp for some few moments.
>
> Holme, *Silver Wreath*, Hitch Account, p.62

Behind this desperate fight along the front barricade and particularly the hospital porch, Lieutenants Chard and Bromhead were again seen demonstrating enormous courage and initiative, actively plugging gaps and reinforcing any perceived weak points in the perimeter defences. Their role became particularly crucial as the Zulus gradually extended the focus of their attacks along the whole of the front wall. At one point it seemed as if the Zulus would even scale the wall traversing the biscuit boxes, so Chard was forced to, 'run back with two or three men to this part of the wall and was immediately joined by Bromhead with two or three more. The enemy stuck to this assault most tenaciously.' (Ibid., Chard Account, p.51)

Two other officers, Corporal Christian Schiess and Acting Assistant Commissary James Dalton, were now emerging as veritable Herculean figures in the midst of the tumult of battle, with Dalton apparently dropping a Zulu warrior every time he fired his rifle. As the Zulus pressed against the front barricades, Chaplain Smith observed the already wounded 'giant' Corporal Scheiss, after emerging from his sick bed in the hospital and incensed when his hat was blown off by a Zulu bullet, commencing a frenzied assault on a group of Zulu cowering beneath the mealie bag wall. Scheiss, he recalled, instantly 'jumped upon the parapet and bayoneted the man, regaining his place, and shot another, and then repeated [sic] his former exploit, climbed up on the sacks and bayoneted a third'. (Lummis, *Smith Diary*, p.52)

Such exceptional demonstrations of military prowess from men like Dalton, Hitch and Schiess must have impressed, if not

*Acting Storekeeper Louis Byrne. (RRWM)*

demoralised, many of the attacking Zulu, whilst, conversely, greatly reinforcing the fighting spirit and morale of their comrades. Even more disheartening for the enemy must have been the overt defiance directed at them even by the more severely wounded British defenders. After Dalton himself was seriously injured whilst firing over the parapet and treated by Surgeon Reynolds for a bullet wound above the right shoulder, he bravely continued to direct the fire of the men around him. His rifle was subsequently handed over to Acting Storekeeper Louis Byrne who 'used it well'. Soon afterwards a dying Corporal Scammell, mortally wounded by a Zulu bullet in his spine, still managed to crawl a short distance from the storehouse to Lieutenant Chard to hand to him the remainder of his valuable cartridges. As Byrne nobly fetched water at the request of the expiring Scammell, he was shot through the head, dying close beside him. Similarly, when Private Hitch and Corporal Allen were also later badly wounded and 'incapacitated from using their rifles', they continued to serve their comrades with ammunition under fire. Comradeship and extreme self-

*The Reverend George Smith, who played such a crucial role in sustaining garrison morale at Rorke's Drift, wearing his campaign medals. (EY)*

*Surgeon James Henry Reynolds, M.B., one of the defenders of Rorke's Drift. (JY)*

sacrifice were undoubtedly the order of the day. (Ibid., Chard Account, p.50)

Non-combatants were also present in the thick of the fight, playing a vital role in maintaining the garrison's logistical supplies of water, food and, above all, ammunition. Surgeon Reynolds and Chaplain Smith were particularly active in supplying fresh ammunition. Smith also offered great comfort and cheer to the weary soldiers on the ramparts, tempered with Christian zeal. Lieutenant Stafford, in conversation with Lieutenant Adendorff, four years after the battle recorded this colourful story of Smith's activities during the siege:

> He (Adendorff) told me that the Reverend W. Smith was a great help. You'll always find that in a tight corner there is a hard case and there was one at Rorke's Drift. This man was cussing all the time. The Reverend Smith went to him and said, 'please my good man stop that cussing. We may shortly have to answer for our sins'. The reply he got was, 'alright minister, you do the praying and I will send the black B's to hell as fast as I can!'
>
> NAM, Stafford Papers

Even General Wolseley, not known for his appreciation of the Rorke's Drift action, expressed his admiration for the 'fighting missionary' of Rorke's Drift, who had 'not fired on a Zulu himself but had gone round our men sending out ammo and telling them to fire low'. (Preston, *Wolseley's South African Diary*, p.145)

It was, however, to take more than religion to save the garrison hospital, now in Dunne's words, 'subjected to the heaviest attack'. At around 6pm, after up to ninety minutes' hard fighting, and with signs of severe overstretch along the extended front perimeter, Chard called 'all the men inside our entrenchment'. Over thirty sick men and a few scattered able-bodied hospital defenders, now faced the full wrath of their Zulu attackers.

## Phase 3: Nadir

The Hospital Fight.

22 January 1879

| | | |
|---|---|---|
| c.6pm | Due both to the ferocity of the main frontal perimeter assaults and costly over-exposure to Zulu sniper fire, Chard orders a tactical retreat to his inner barricade |
| c.6–8pm | The fight for the hospital rages. The Zulu attackers set fire to the thatched roof. Four of the eleven Rorke's Drift VCs are specifically won here for both its gallant internal defence and eventual evacuation – Privates Hook, William and Robert Jones, and John Williams |

We were pinned like rats in a hole.

Private Hook, *Silver Wreath*, p.64

*Private John Williams VC.*
*(RRWM)*

Dusk fell. As the night closed in, the struggle decisively deepened and the battle for Rorke's Drift entered a new, even more deadly phase. The British retreat to the inner 'biscuit box' enclosure from the hospital area, and the subsequent Zulu infiltration of the hospital, represented the most critical stage of the battle for both sides. For Dabulamanzi and his subordinate *indunas*, it represented their greatest opportunity, not only to fatally divide the garrison, but also to 'break its back' by over-running the retreating red line. Nearly one-quarter of Chard's men were literally 'pinned like rats in a hole' in the now isolated hospital – over thirty sick and barely half a dozen able-bodied men – Privates William and Robert Jones, Robert Cole, Henry Hook, William Horrigan, John and Joseph Williams and John Waters. As the dispersed red line rapidly retreated to the safety of the biscuit box barricade, the Zulu mounted a massive attack designed to both over-run the hospital and annihilate the retreating soldiers. With the 24th Regulars falling back, Chaplain Smith observed, at around 6pm, the emergence of scores of Zulus who jumped over the abandoned mealie bags to get into the building. Private Hitch, caught in the middle of this major onslaught, was horribly aware of the potential for disaster at this point:

> Again this was just before they tried to fire the other building, they seemed to me as if they had made up their minds to take Rorke's Drift with this rush. They rushed up madly, not withstanding the heavy loss they had already suffered.
>
> Holme, *Silver Wreath*, Hitch Account, p.62

Many Zulu were, indeed, shot down by combined fire, emanating from both the hospital and the soldiers re-positioned on the new inner defences, comprising Chard's biscuit box barricade in which 'nearly every man perished in that fatal leap but they rushed to their death like demons, yelling out the war cry of "Usuto, Usuto!"'. (Lummis, *Smith Diary*, p.53) A good many other Zulu undoubtedly closed with the momentarily disorientated defenders carrying out their retreat from the outer perimeter, and 'it was in this struggle' that Private Hitch was shot. Hitch, defending a position on the right of the second line of defence with Bromhead in the centre, was exposed to crossfire. He recalled his deadly encounter with the Zulu as he desperately tried to fend off several assegai thrusts:

> They pressed us very hard, several of them mounting the barricade. I knew this one had got his rifle presented at me but at the same time I had got my hands full in front and I was at the present when he shot me through my right shoulder blade and [it] passed through my shoulder which splintered the shoulder bone very much.
>
> Holme, *Silver Wreath*, Hitch Account, p.62

Hitch was the last of six men shot in this exposed area (four killed and two wounded). Once again the irrepressible Bromhead arrived to save the day: 'I tried to keep my feet, but could not, he could have assegaied me had not Bromhead shot him with his revolver.' The following brief exchange between Bromhead and Hitch yet again illustrated the high morale, strength of comradeship and fighting spirit which pervaded this tiny garrison:

> Bromhead seemed sorry when he saw me down bleeding so freely, saying 'Mate, I am very sorry to see you down'. I was not down more than a few minutes, stripping [to] my shirt sleeves with my waist belt on and valise straps. I put my wounded arm under my waist belt. I was able to make another stand, getting Bromhead's revolver and, with his assistance in loading it, I managed very well with it.
>
> Holme, *Silver Wreath*, Hitch Account, p.62

As if this latest Zulu 'thunder clap' was not enough, the defenders were dealt another major psychological blow. After penetrating the hospital entrance, several intrepid Zulu attackers proceeded to fire the thatch at the furthest end of the hospital. The thirty-odd

*A depiction of an incident during the hospital fight, revealing the savagery of the struggle. (JY)*

men occupying the hospital were now trapped in a maze of tiny cramped rooms with, in many cases, extremely thin walls and doors, and worst of all, no communicating corridor. They were in a 'terrible plight'. In Hook's words, it:

> meant that we were either to be massacred, or burned alive, or get out of the building. To get out seemed impossible; for if we left the hospital by the only door which had been left open, we should instantly fall into the midst of the Zulu.
>
> Holme, *Silver Wreath*, Hook Account, p.64

This dilemma, largely reflecting the poor state of the hospital's inner defences, formed an interesting focal point of Chard's later battle report. Within this report, in a rare moment of criticism of his own men, Chard pinpointed a glaring weakness in the hospital defence arrangements:

> All this time the enemy had been attempting to fire the hospital and had at length set fire to its roof and got in at the far end. I had tried to impress upon the men in the hospital the necessity for making a communication right through the building – unfortunately this was not done. Probably at the time the men could not see the necessity, and doubtless also there was no time to do it.
>
> Holme, *Silver Wreath*, Chard Account, p.51

Chard lamented the absence of his cherished Royal Engineer sappers who earlier that morning he had already unknowingly left to be massacred at Isandlwana camp, and who could have effectively transformed the inner hospital defences. He chose his words carefully:

> Without in the least detracting from the gallant fellows who defended the hospital and, I hope, I shall not be misunderstood in saying so, I have always regretted, as I did then, the absence

of my poor sappers, who had only left that morning for Isandlwana and arrived there just to be killed.

Ibid.

Despite these defensive shortfalls, the subsequent heroic struggle and defence of the hospital was to provide a crucial turning point in the fortunes of the garrison. In Colonel Whitton's words:

there were gallant deeds done at Rorke's Drift that day but for courage and devotion to duty nothing can exceed the conduct of the half dozen Privates of the 24th Regiment left, as the garrison of the doomed building.

Whitton, *Deeds*

Gunner Howard, located with sick patient Private Adams in the far front corner room, arguably the most exposed position of the hospital defences, could only offer limited resistance after the Zulus had burst in through the front entrance porch. In the ensuing mêlée, Howard took the opportunity to run out of the front of the hospital and managed to conceal himself in the long grass on the other side of the stone wall below the front parapet. In company with a dead pig and four deceased horses, shot earlier where they were tethered, he lay undetected throughout the night, the Zulu masses swirling over and above him. It was to be the first of several miraculous escapes. The less daring Private Adams stayed and paid with his life, shot or assegaied in the room itself. Surgeon Reynolds later elaborated on his terrible fate, recalling that Adams, while 'well able to move about... could not be persuaded to leave his temporary refuge in a small room and face the danger of an attempt to escape to the laager'. He paid with his life. (AMCM, Reynolds Report)

Private Hook – who provided the most detailed account of this phase of the battle – was able, through a succession of gallant deeds, to save the lives of many sick patients. Occupying his post in a room at the far end of the hospital with Privates Thomas, 'Old King' Cole and one sick African patient, Hook was subjected to the full terror of the hungry flames licking the thatched roof above him, combined with the nightmarish sounds of furious Zulu pounding against the walls and door outside. In later years, he vividly recalled the 'extraordinary rattle as the bullets struck the biscuit boxes and queer thuds as they plumped into the bags of mealies'. Hook's previous combat experience undoubtedly helped him to control his nerves in this critical situation, the 'whiz and rip of the assegais' reminding him of his recent 'experiences in the Kaffir campaigns of 1877 to 1878'. (Holme, *Silver Wreath*, Hook Account, p.64)

Worse was to follow. Soon, Private Hook became the only able-bodied defender left in his room, as the nerve of Private Cole finally broke. After abruptly informing Hook he 'was not going to stay', he went outside 'and was instantly killed by the Zulu'. His subsequent death was witnessed by Chaplain Smith:

> A whisper passes round amongst the men; 'Poor Old king Cole is killed'. He had reached the front wall where, 'a bullet passed through his head, and then struck the next man upon the bridge of his nose…
>
> Lummis, *Smith Diary*, p.52

Hook's only company now was the injured African patient, apparently a native of Umlunga's tribe who had been shot through the thigh during the earlier fight at Sihayo's kraal. His leg was broken and he kept crying out 'take my bandages off so that I can come!' Chaplain Smith recalled the bravery of this particular man who defiantly cried out that he 'was not afraid of the Zulus and wanted a gun'. (Ibid.)

Astonishingly, Private Hook continued to be unperturbed by this terrible predicament, as 'it was impossible to do anything but fight, and I blazed away as hard as I could'. His defence of this room was short-lived, however, as flames and dense choking smoke crept in the room and his post became unsustainable. Hook was forced to exit 'by means of the front door to join his comrades, Privates

Connolly and eight patients in an adjoining room'. Tragically, it proved impossible to take the African patient with him and he was left, in Hook's words, 'to an awful fate but his death was at any rate a merciful one'. Hook heard the Zulus briefly interrogate him but he was apparently killed as he 'tried to tear off his bandages and escape'. (Holme, *Silver Wreath*, Hook Account, p.64)

Next door, for over an hour, Privates William Horrigan, John and Joseph Williams had been hard put to defend their room and the five patients in their care against the fierce assaults of their Zulu attackers. A failure of ammunition apparently sealed the fate of several of these men. In the thick smoke, the escaping Hook thus came across a distressed Private John Williams, who blurted out the news of Private Joseph William's terrible fate: 'the Zulus are swarming all over the place. They have dragged Joseph Williams out and killed him.'. With no cartridges left, Joseph Williams had, in fact, been grabbed by several enraged Zulu who had promptly disembowelled him alive in front of his horrified comrades. Poor Private Joseph Williams had probably paid dearly for his earlier successes, the historian Moodie recording the later discovery of up to fourteen Zulu dead below his firing position outside his window and others along his line of fire. (Moodie, *Moodie's Zulu War*, p.82) Zulu vengeance had been swift. Within minutes, Private Horrigan was also stabbed to death and two helpless patients, including Private Garrett Hayden, were assegaied in their beds. Drummer Hayden was later found stabbed in sixteen places, his belly cut open in two places and part of his cheek cut off. Meanwhile, the surviving Private John Williams, with two patients, had managed to break through the thin mud wall of his room using a navvy's pick, thereby achieving a successful link-up with the beleaguered Private Hook.

Besieged by Zulus approaching from both outside the back wall and now emerging from the two rooms abandoned by Private Hook and John Williams, the 'fire fight' within the hospital reached a new intensity. In such a confined space, the mode of fighting was again largely reduced to assegai, bayonet and rifle butt. Horrific injuries were inflicted upon both defender and attacker alike. Hook himself had a narrow escape, as assegais 'kept whizzing toward us' and one struck him in the front of his helmet which 'tilted back under the blow' making 'the spear lose its power so that I escaped with a scalp wound'. While this 'did not trouble me much then', it 'has often caused me illness since'. (Holme, *Silver Wreath*, Hook Account, p.64) As Hook fought desperately to defend the exposed doorway, the ever resourceful Private John Williams again hacked through a side wall to reach the next room where eight sick patients and Privates Connolly, Savage, R.C. Cole, Waters and others were located.

Private Waters of 1/24th soon opted for an equally daring escape strategy. Teaming up with the already injured Private Beckett, he discovered, in the adjoining room, an ingenious place of refuge. Five months after the battle he recounted his experiences to the *Cambrian Newspaper*:

> While I was there, I took refuge in a cupboard and Private Beckett, an invalid, came with me. As they (Zulu) were going out (after firing the roof) I killed many of them and as I could not stay there long, the place being suffocating, I put on a black coat which I found in a cupboard and which must have belonged to Mr Witt, and ran out in the long grass and lay down. The Zulus must have thought I was one of their dead comrades as they were all around me and some trod on me.
>
> Holme, *Silver Wreath*, Waters Account, p.59

Lieutenant Chard, interviewing Waters after the battle, was able to complete his story, relating how Waters eventually found his way to the cook-house where he found 'the Zulus were occupying this and firing at us from the wall nearest us'. It was, 'too late to retreat', so Waters, 'crept softly to the fireplace and, standing up in the chimney, blackened his hands and face with the soot. He remained there until the Zulus left.' (Holme, *Silver Wreath*, Chard Account, p.53) His sick colleague, Beckett, was less fortunate. Evacuating the cupboard about half an hour earlier, he was

*Private William Jones VC. (RRWM)*

'assegaied right through the stomach'. Discovered next morning, he died soon after frantic treatment from Surgeon Reynolds who did 'all he could to save him but did not succeed'. (Holme, *Silver Wreath*, Waters Account, p.59)

The ensuing epic struggle in the back rooms was again graphically recorded by Private Hook who, like Hitch, was one of the few survivors to record their face-to-face encounters with the enemy:

> Only one man at a time could get in at the door. A big Zulu sprang forward and seized my rifle and I tore it free and, slipping a cartridge in, I shot him point blank. Time after time the Zulus gripped the muzzle and tried to tear the rifle from my grasp, and time after time I wrenched it back because I had a better grip than they had.
>
> Holme, *Silver Wreath*, Hook Account, p.64

All this time, Private John Williams was dragging the sick patients through the adjoining wall to the next ward which faced the hill and which was occupied by Privates Robert and William Jones and about seven patients, including a semi-conscious, fever-ridden Sergeant Robert Maxfield. Maxfield and another sick patient, Private John Connolly (called mistakenly Conley by Hook), who suffered from a partial dislocation of his left knee in a wagon-loading accident, posed a severe problem in the evacuation procedure. Connolly's heavy build forced a desperate Hook to drag him so violently through the narrow hole that his leg was consequently re-broken. There was, as Hook recalled, 'no help for it'. He continued: 'As soon as we left the room, the Zulus burst in with furious cries of disappointment and rage.' Sadly, the delirious Sergeant Maxfield, who had stubbornly refused to be either dressed or rescued, had to be left behind and was brutally stabbed to death in his bed. Years later his terrible fate continued to haunt members of the Rorke's Drift garrison:

> We had to leave him there to be killed. Ah! Poor fellow! And sometimes, thinking it over, I cannot help feeling that I might somehow or other have devised escape for him. I can't help feeling it. But it is hard to think coolly in a rush of that kind.
>
> AMCM, Reynolds Report

Private John Jobbins also long lamented the death of 'poor Sergeant Maxfield' who, he observed, was 'insane' and was 'burnt alive or killed and then burnt'. (Holme, *Silver Wreath*, Jobbins Account, p.65) Private Robert Jones did in fact return in a desperate last attempt to save Sergeant Maxfield but, as flames and smoke encircled the room, he could only watch helplessly as Maxfield was killed.

In this final defensive position, a small window situated at the end of the hospital, presented the only feasible means of escape. Beyond the window lay a courtyard requiring a 30-odd yard perilous dash to rejoin the rest of the anxious garrison, who were now fully entrenched in their new defensive positions behind the line of biscuit boxes. There was no alternative to this potential ordeal, as the Zulus had deeply penetrated the burning hospital and casualties had rapidly mounted during this room-to-room struggle for survival. Already 'one poor fellow', Jenkins, prematurely venturing through one of the holes, had been 'also seized and dragged away'. (Lummis, Smith Diary, p.52) As the two Joneses heroically 'kept at it with bullet and bayonet', the remaining men alternatively dashed, hobbled, or even crawled across the 'courtyard of death'. One man, Trooper Hunter of the Natal Mounted Police, inexplicably and fatally hesitated. Hunter, a 'very tall man', clearly bewildered and possibly suffering from battle shock, or, as Chard concluded, 'dazed by the glare of the burning hospital and the firing that was going on all around… was assegaied before our eyes, the Zulu who killed him immediately afterwards falling'. (Holme, *Silver Wreath*, Chard Account, p.51)

Surgeon Reynolds provided a different account of Hunter's demise, describing how, reaching the inner defences, he was 'shot dead while crossing over the biscuit boxes by… fire from the enemy from behind mealie sacks'. Harry Lugg recalled his fellow trooper as 'ill with rheumatism and being assegaied in the kidneys and exhibiting five wounds in the chest', although most of these stab wounds were probably inflicted later as the Zulus re-occupied the courtyard. Fortunately, Trooper Hunter was the only man to be killed in this desperate retreat across the hospital courtyard. (AMCM, Reynolds Report; Emery, *Red Soldier*, Lugg Account, p.132)

Three other patients involved in this final dash to relative safety experienced notably difficult exits. Corporal J.H. Mayer, NNC, earlier wounded by an assegai at the Sihayo kraal skirmish, Royal Artilleryman Bombardier T. Lewis, suffering a swollen leg and thigh from a wagon accident, and patient Trooper R. Green, NMP, were reduced to crawling on their hands and knees. Chaplain Smith recalled their painful ordeal:

> The window being high up and the Zulus already within the room behind them, each man had a fall in escaping and then

had to crawl (for none of them could walk) through the enemy's fire to inside the entrenchment.

Lummis, Smith Diary, p.54

For poor Trooper Green the pain was surely magnified as he was struck by a spent bullet. After successfully crossing to the inner barricade the surviving sick and wounded were rapidly escorted to the safety of the storehouse verandah where Surgeon Reynolds again excelled himself by doing 'everything he could for them' in the midst of continual 'heavy fire and clouds of assegais'. (Holme, *Silver Wreath*, Hook Account, p.64)

# Phase 4: The Final Ordeal

| | | |
|---|---|---|
| **22–23 January** | c.7–10pm | Zulu assaults against the front barricades are exposed to intense British fire by the light of the burning hospital. Heavy Zulu casualties result. Zulus refocus on inner perimeter, especially front of the storehouse. Fresh Zulu assault launched against the cattle kraal at the eastern end of the post and British defenders largely driven out |
| | c.10pm–2am | Fighting continues with varying intensity. Successful British foray to recover water cart from outside inner barricade. Construction of the final mealie bag redoubt |
| **23 January** | c.4am | Final shots and probing attacks by Zulus |
| | c.4.30am | Around dawn during this protracted lull, Chard sends out search and reconnaissance parties to check Zulu presence, collect Zulu weaponry and, to reduce fire risk by stripping thatch from storehouse roof |
| | c.5am | False alarm over British reinforcements |
| | c.7am | Parties of Zulu observed to south-east but retire some minutes later |
| | c.8am | Arrival of Lord Chelmsford's relief column |

The rest is just a story of sticking to it. We stood up face to face, white and black, and blazed at each other... they broke in on us and we drove them back. They hammered at us and we struck the hammer up. And then God sent the night and the flag was still flying.

Reynolds, 'How VCs are Won'

For the rest of the garrison, only yards away from the burning hospital, the situation was clearly one of great stress and anxiety, coupled with a profound sense of helplessness. As they watched their compatriots struggling to reach the inner barricade, all they could do was to provide covering fire or reach over the biscuit boxes in order to pull their comrades to safety. However, as the fight continued, the Zulus had, by firing the hospital, unwittingly bequeathed a small but significant tactical advantage to their British enemies. As Sergeant George Smith later revealed: 'the light from the burning hospital was of the greatest of service to our men, lighting up the scene for hundreds of yards around', although, 'before 10pm it had burnt itself out'.

*Post-battle view from the front. Only one or two trees have survived the siege. The Oskarsberg terraces behind the post proved a fertile ground for scores of Zulu snipers. The depression in the foreground may have been the site of a mass Zulu grave. (EY)*

For two or three hours at least, it provided a terrible 'killing ground', as their incredibly brave Zulu assailants, 'lighted themselves for us in lurid flames against the darkness, and we poured in death upon them with a rush that swept them away'.

During the couple of hours after around 10pm, further major assaults were launched against the shrunken British perimeter. Again showing his great tactical awareness, Chard later recognised this period as the probable final test or reckoning for his garrison.

The exceptional determination of Dabulamanzi, his commanders and their regiments was clearly signified by the decision to sustain the battle through the hours of darkness. Night fighting was a rare Zulu tactic and was never repeated again during the course of the Anglo-Zulu War. Indeed, the decision of the Zulu command to persevere after several hours of almost continuous fighting throws considerable doubt upon recent theories alleging their role to be merely one of an opportunist raiding party.

Huddled behind their mealie bag and biscuit box barricades, the garrison were made even more aware of their dire predicament and complete encirclement as they heard in the darkness, the demoralising sounds of their exultant Zulu protagonists, wrecking the camp of B Company. Amidst the orgy of looting, an amused Chard observed the strenuous efforts of his batman, Driver Robson, who persistently fired on one particular group of Zulu plunderers in a futile attempt to keep them off a wagon containing 'our things'.

Such brief lighter moments belied the unrelenting grim situation confronting the tiny British garrison as Dabulamanzi launched his final wave of assaults to try to finish them off. This time, the focus of the Zulu commanders was on the cattle kraal and the store building, fire from which had earlier caused considerable casualties in their ranks. In their final murderous assault, still exposed by the dying flames of the hospital, the Zulu paid a heavy price. Trooper Harry Lugg recalled:

> At about 10 they came on in tremendous force, sweeping the fellows before them and causing them to retreat to the store.

But Providence favoured us. The thatched roof… burst out in flames… and made it as light as day and, before they had time to retreat, we were pouring the bullets into them like hail. We could see them falling in scores.

Emery, *Red Soldier*, Lugg Account, p.132

Gunner Howard was more ebullient:

When the flames burst out it was all the better for us for we could see the niggers [sic] and their movements although they could not see us. Didn't we give it to them then anyhow.

Emery, *Red Soldier*, Howard Account, p.134

By midnight Zulu morale and energy was clearly faltering, as the pace of the attacks slowed up and more time was taken to regroup. Private Hook recalled the futility of such brave Zulu forays increasingly punctuated by retreats into the bush for morale-building war ceremonies:

We could see them coming and they could not rush us and take us by surprise from any point… so they went away and had ten or fifteen minutes of war-dance. This roused them again and their excitement was so intense that the ground fairly seemed to shake. Then when they were goaded to the highest pitch they would hurl themselves at us again.

Holme, *Silver Wreath*, Hook Account, p.64

The garrison itself was also rapidly weakening, as individual Zulu attackers came close to setting fire to the store roof, a tactic which could have proved disastrous as it would have deprived them of the one remaining area of complete shelter. Fortunately, all the attacks failed, with one intrepid Zulu warrior being shot, 'I believe by Lieutenant Adendorff' just as the light was 'almost touching the thatch'. (Holme, *Silver Wreath*, Chard Account, p.51)

## ZULU WAR RITUALS

Important ceremonies preceded deployment for war, the regiments performing certain rituals in front of the king lasting up to two or three days. These 'superstitious practices' included ritual washing in the river, the consumption of doctored bull flesh and even ritual vomiting. On the third day the warriors were 'sprinkled' with medicine by their doctors.

The potential for disaster presented by such incidents forced Chard to reorganise and order one more key tactical change – the construction of a final redoubt, both to act as a sanctuary for the more seriously wounded and ultimately to provide a final firing position. In his report, Reynolds recognised Chard's construction of this 'cone shaped stack of mealies' as a 'last stand' strategy. Chard, in his view, had again showed great foresight and 'shined in resource' by 'anticipating the Zulus making one more united dash for the fort and possibly making an entrance'. It was a strenuous task, as assisted by Assistant Commissary Officer Dunne and other men, the core of an immense stack of mealies was rapidly decapitated and a number of sacks removed from the heart of what remained. This task was 'hard work for the bags of mealie weighed 200 pounds each', which created a sheltered space 'sufficient to accommodate 40 men and in a position to make good shooting', as well as to provide a second elevated line of fire. It was, apparently a surreal period in the battle, as 'overhead small birds, disturbed from their nests by the turmoil and smoke flew hither and thither confusedly', a scene that is now more commonly evoked by the First World War trenches, where soldiers were often distracted by such small comforting signs of nature amidst the horror and carnage. ( Dunne, *Waggoner*)

The Zulu attackers enjoyed a greater degree of success along the eastern perimeter outside the permanent wall of the cattle kraal. After a protracted struggle and several repulses of their

Zulu attackers, the exhausted British defenders were slowly forced back, inch by inch, to the middle and then to the inner wall. The Zulus then rapidly occupied the middle wall as the British were forced to abandon it. However, here the position was at last stabilised, as the middle wall proved:

> too high for them to use it to effectively to fire over and a Zulu no sooner showed his head over it than he was dropped, being so close it was almost impossible to miss him.
>
> Holme, *Silver Wreath*, Chard Account, p.52

By now, the defenders had experienced nearly eight hours of almost continual fighting and the heavy toll on men and equipment was becoming starkly apparent. Lieutenant Bromhead, continually touring the positions of his men, was particularly worried about the high expenditure of fire, 'keeping a strict eye on the ammunition and telling the men not to waste one round'. (Holmes, *Silver Wreath*, Hitch Account, p.62) Numbers of the vital weapon, the otherwise 'fine' Martini-Henry rifles, were also showing ominous signs of wear and tear:

> We did so much firing that [they] became hot, and the brass of the cartridges softened, the result being that the barrels got very foul and the cartridge chamber jammed. My own rifle was jammed several times!
>
> Holme, *Silver Wreath*, Hook Account , p.64

Even some of the otherwise 'very fine' three-sided 'lunger' bayonets, with their deadly long thin blades, were proving to be of indifferent quality and had:

> either twisted or bent badly. Several were like that after the fight; but some terrible thrusts were given, and I saw dead Zulu who had been pinned to the ground by the bayonets going through them.
>
> Holme, *Silver Wreath*, Hook Account , p.64

100

## The Battlefield: What Actually Happened?

The British defenders were themselves exhibiting significant signs of battle fatigue. In the early hours of the morning, an already seriously wounded Private Hitch, wearily leaning against the biscuit boxes, recalled his somewhat fatalistic conversation with a fellow 24th soldier, Private Deacon. Deacon asked:

> 'Fred, when it comes to the last shall I shoot you?' I declined, 'no, they have very nearly done for me and they can finish me right out when it comes to the last'. Hitch added, tellingly, 'I don't remember much after that'.
>
> Holme, *Silver Wreath*, Hitch Account , p.62

Water became a pressing need, and for many their desperate thirst was undoubtedly enhanced by the terrible psychological and emotional stresses of such unrelenting combat. Unfortunately, in the rush to retreat from the hospital, the water cart had been left isolated beyond the inner barricades and alongside the hospital wall. Private Hitch soon became so thirsty and faint that he 'could not do much'. As in the hospital, Private Hook was to again emerge as a saviour of the situation. Having taken up his new post alongside a barricade in the inner fort area, where two men had already earlier been shot, Hook, at around midnight, felt compelled to take drastic action:

> All this time the sick and wounded were crying for water but it was just by the deserted hospital and we could not hope to get it until the day broke when the Zulus might begin to lose heart and to stop in their mad rushes. But we could not bear the cries any longer and three or four of us jumped over the boxes and ran and fetched some water in.
>
> Holme, *Silver Wreath*, Hook Account, pp.64–5

For the scores of dying and wounded Zulu littered inside and immediately outside perimeter, and effectively isolated from their comrades, the situation must have been far worse. At least their comrades in the bush would presumably have had a ready supply of water from the nearby Buffalo, or Mzinyathi River.

The collapse of the hospital defences and the occupation of most of the cattle kraal defensive area represented the high tide of Zulu successes. By midnight, probably demoralised or crippled by such terrible losses, the intensity of their attacks took a rapid downturn. Lieutenant Chard recalled the noticeable reduction in pressure during the early hours of the morning of the 23rd:

> About midnight or a little after, the fire slackened, and after that, although they kept us constantly on the alert by feigning, as before, to come on at different points, the fire was of a desultory character… a few shots from the Zulus replied to by our men – again silence broken by the same thing repeated.
>
> Holme, *Silver Wreath*, Chard Account, p.52

There was, however, no possibility of relaxing with the ever-present danger of a renewed Zulu attack. Walter Dunne, for instance, felt curiously unnerved by the long pregnant silences after midnight:

> Broken only by the words of command of the Zulu leaders which sounded strangely close. How we longed to know what they said! Every man was then on the alert straining eyes and ears to detect the rush which was sure to follow, only to be checked each time by a withering volley.
>
> AMCM, Dunne, *Waggoner*, Reminiscences

It was in fact highly fortuitous for the garrison that no major Zulu assault took place during these last fateful hours. In his subsequent report on the battle, Chard strikingly revealed that by early morning, while each man 'still had a good supply of ammunition in his pouches we had only a box and a half besides' or about 900 rounds. (Holme, *Silver Wreath*, Chard Account, p.53)

In fact, at about this time, Chard had felt compelled to send a frightened fugitive 'Kaffir' messenger to Helpmekaar, outlining his predicament and urgently calling for aid. For Dabulamanzi, it had been the great missed opportunity and one final major assault before dawn might have proved successful. It was not to be.

The garrison put these periods of lull in the fighting to great use. Lieutenant Chard, again demonstrating his endless energy, detailed a working party to rebuild the strength of the remaining defences, mainly by raising the walls and placing sacks of mealie on top of the biscuit boxes, and also to reconnoitre and collect abandoned Zulu weapons. In a wise move, the thatch was removed from the Commissariat Store 'to avoid being burnt out in case of another attack'. (Holme, *Silver Wreath*, Chard Account, p.52)

Patrolling around the perimeter, 'collecting the arms and ammunition of the dead Zulus', Chard was both horrified and intrigued by their odd dispositions and the terrible damage inflicted by Martini-Henry rounds:

> Some of the bullet wounds were very curious. One man's head was split open, exactly as if done with an axe. Another had been hit just between the eyes, the bullet carrying away the whole of the back of his head, leaving his face perfect, as though it were a mask, only disfigured by the small hole made by the bullet passing through. One of the wretches we found one hand grasping a bench that had been dragged from the hospital, and sustained thus in the position we found him, while in the other hand he still clutched the knife with which he had mutilated one of our poor fellows, over whom he was still leaning.
>
> Holme, *Silver Wreath*, Chard Account, p.52

Other parties were detailed to collect and destroy the scores of muskets and assegais strewn across the ground, while a third party had 'the painful task of decently laying out our dead in a corner of the enclosure'. Walking around, Dunne found 'everywhere dead Zulus – all ring kops that is married men who alone wear a black ring woven into the hair of the head'. (AMCM, Dunne, *Waggoner*, Reminiscences) The cold light of dawn revealed distressing scenes in what must have seemed like a landscape from hell:

> The scene we beheld was a strange and sad one! On one side stood the blackened walls and still smouldering ruins of the hospital. Around it and in front of that side of the barrier lay the bodies of Zulus in rows, as if literally mown down, showing how brave had been the assault and how unerring the fire that had laid them low. Inside were our own dead comrades – stark and cold, one still kneeling in a natural position at the wall – while the wounded excited pity by their sufferings patiently borne. The ground was strewn with trampled grain which had run from the bags pierced by bullet or assegai, and every face was black with smoke and sweat of toil and battle.
>
> AMCM, Dunne, *Waggoner*, Reminiscences

Commandant Hamilton-Browne was after the battle similarly appalled by the scenes of carnage:

> The hospital was still smouldering and the stench from the burning flesh of the dead inside was very bad... some of our sick and wounded had been burned inside the hospital and a number of Zulus had been also killed inside of the building itself... a few of our men... had... in trying to escape been killed, their bodies also being ripped and much mutilated... A few dead horses lay about, either killed by the assegai or by the bullets of the defenders, and I wondered why they had not been driven away before the fighting began. One thing I noticed and that was the extraordinary way in which the majority of Zulus lay. I had been over a good many battlefields and seen very many men who had been killed in action but I had never seen men lie in this position. They seemed to have dropped on their elbows and knees and remained like that with their knees drawn up to their chins. One huge fellow

who must have been, in life, seven feet high lay on his back with his heels on the top of the parapet and his head nearly touching the ground, the rest of his body supported by a heap of his dead comrades.

Hamilton-Browne, *Lost Legionary*

The sense of horror which pervaded the garrison was only equalled by a sense of gratitude for their survival so far. As the severely wounded hospital survivor Private Waters put it:

I got up at daybreak having expected that every minute my life would be taken and then saw my comrades on top of the mealie sacks and I said 'thank God I have got my life.'

Holme, *Silver Wreath*, Waters Account, p.59

The battle was, however, not quite over – it was still to be a couple of hours before relief would finally arrive. One false alarm occurred early that morning (at 5am, according to Dunne). Several lookouts spotted a cloud of dust on the road some miles away in the direction of the British outpost of Helpmekaar. Some claimed they saw red coats and the ensuing loud cheers apparently astonished their Zulu assailants and, according to Dunne, even caused 'the enemy to pause' as if to 'know what it meant', but sadly the dust was dispersed by the wind and the longed-for help never materialised. (AMCM, Dunne, *Waggoner*, Reminiscences) The blow to garrison morale must have been considerable. Later, after the battle, Chard speculated on the circumstances surrounding this event:

It is very strange that this report should have arisen among us for the two companies of 24th from Helpmekaar did come down to the foot of the hill, but not, I believe, in sight of us. They marched back to Helpmekaar on the report of Rorke's Drift having fallen.

Holme, *Silver Wreath*, Chard Account, p.52

The Official History confirms also how two companies of the 24th had approached the garrison but, seeing flames from the post and presuming disaster, had promptly retreated back to their Helpmekaar post.

At around 7am, another sighting, this time of a large group of the enemy, provided a further test for the garrisons mettle. A 'large body' of the enemy appeared on hills to the south-west. As the signallers on the store roof frantically alerted the rest of the garrison to their presence, Hook recalled the 'awful time of suspense… we looked everywhere for sign of relief but saw nothing and our hearts sank'. (Holme, *Silver Wreath*, Hook Account, p.65)

By contrast, Chard, using his past experience, was convinced of the unlikelihood of any major Zulu attack:

> I thought at the time they were going to attack us, but what I know from Zulus, and also of the number we put 'hors de combat', I do not think so. I think that they came up on the high ground to observe Lord Chelmsford's advance; from there they could see the Column long before it came in sight of us.
>
> Holme, *Silver Wreath*, Chard Account, p.52

The garrison was astonished by one last admirable act of enemy defiance:

> One Zulu had remained in the Kraal and fired a shot among us (without doing any damage) as we stood on the walls, and he ran off over the hill and in the direction of the river – although many shots were fired at him as he ran, I am glad to say the plucky fellow got off.
>
> Holme, *Silver Wreath*, Chard Account, p.52

It was the last moment of tension, and at about 8am, as the enemy disappeared again, Chelmsford's relief column came into sight. The terrible ordeal for the Rorke's Drift garrison was at last over.

# AFTER THE BATTLE

## Relief

> We broke into roar after roar of cheering, waving red coats and
> white helmets… we cheered again and again.
>> Holme, *Silver Wreath*, Hook Account, p.65

> I thank you all for your gallant defence.
>> Lord Chelmsford, *RLCM*, Dunne Account

The sight of Chelmsford's approaching relief column did not
immediately inspire confidence within the Rorke's Drift garrison.
Some suspected it was a typical Zulu ruse. Surgeon Reynolds was
one of the sceptics:

> For a long time and even after red coats were distinguished
> through our field glasses, we believed them to be the enemy,
> some of them perhaps dressed in the kits of those who had
> fallen at Isandhlwana.
>> AMCM, Reynolds Report

Lieutenant Chard also shared his initial caution as the column
came into sight:

*Lieutenant Colonel John Crealock's sketch of the relief of Rorke's Drift*

> There were a great many of our native levies with the Column, and the number of red coats seemed so few that, at first, we had grave doubts that the force approaching was the enemy.
>
> Holme, *Silver Wreath*, Chard Account, p.53

Such concerns permeated through to the rank and file of the garrison. As Private Hook put it:

> We saw their flags going wildly. What was it? Everybody was mad with anxiety to know whether it could be friends to relieve us, or more Zulus to destroy us. We watched the flags flapping, and then learnt that signals were being made in reply. We knew we were safe and that friends were marching up to us.
>
> Holme, *Silver Wreath*, Hook Account , p.65

Thus, with the help of an improvised white flag and an exchange of signals, the wonderful moment of relief finally dawned.

Nevertheless, after so many false alarms, Reynolds waited until the last minute – not until the mounted infantry in the advance party had 'crossed the Buffalo Drift' was he and others totally 'convinced of our relief'. Private Jobbins expressed his profound relief and sense of security in simple but telling words:

> We did not at first recognise them, but after a bit we could see the welcome red coats retiring on us from the other unfortunate camp. Then we all gave a hearty cheer, as we felt safe when we were altogether.
>
> Holme, *Silver Wreath*, Jobbins Account, p.65

Private Hook was equally joyful: 'there was not a living soul who was not thankful to find that the Zulus had had enough of it and were disappearing over the hill to the south-west.' (Holmes, *Silver Wreath*, Hook Account, p.65)

The approaching column, having seen the glow of the burning hospital and anticipating another massacre, were extremely tense after their miserable journey to Rorke's Drift from the wrecked Isandlwana camp earlier that morning. Astonishingly, on their journey they had experienced a head-on but strangely bloodless encounter with thousands of retreating Zulu who had streamed past them on the left side of the road from Isandlwana to Rorke's Drift. Lieutenant Archibald Berkeley Milne RN accordingly reported that, within 3 miles of the Drift, 'the enemy were seen in large bodies (some three to four thousand) returning from the river'. (PRO ADM 16486, Milne Report)

Both weary, demoralised columns passed each other in relative silence, the Zulu and their walking wounded painfully exiting from Rorke's Drift in defeat and the traumatised British column mistakenly believing they were a victorious *impi* who had just sacked the post. Consequently neither side had any inclination to fight. Lieutenant Harford vividly recalled this incredible stand-off between these two erstwhile bitter enemies:

Contrary to all expectations, Dabulamanzi made no attempt whatever to interfere with the Column, though some hundreds of his warriors sat or stood within a few yards of us on the right of the road, simply gazing at us like sightseers at a revue… I… and… many others were absolutely dumbfounded at this extraordinary spectacle and could scarcely believe our eyes. Personally, I felt very suspicious about it all and thought a trap was being laid, especially as a few hundred yards below the Buffalo River, great masses of Zulu were coming from Rorke's Drift who could easily have swept up the hills, joined Dabulamanzi's men and come down like an avalanche from the rear on our straggling column.

Harford, *Zulu War Journal*, p.35

The first glimpse of the Rorke's Drift Garrison was probably the most traumatic moment. Lieutenant Harford again relates the story:

As we approached the Drift and reached the hill overlooking the river and the post, the excitement became intense, all eyes were strained and field-glasses raised, to see if there was any sign of life in the fort. Then, as we drew nearer, a man was seen on the bared roof of one of the buildings, signalling with a flag, which was hailed with a tremendous cheer from the whole Column as we knew then that the garrison had not been wiped out.

Harford, *Zulu War Journal*, p.36

As the column came into sight at around 8am (8.15am by Milne's more precise calculation), the last of the Zulu on the Shiyane or Oskarsberg Hill disappeared again to the south-west. The first men to arrive at the post were Major Cecil Russell and Lieutenant Walsh. They led sections of the mounted infantry who were duly 'received by us with a hearty cheer'. Chelmsford and his staff soon followed, literally galloping up to the fort. Chelmsford, still deeply traumatised by the earlier loss of his camp, 'thanked all of us with much emotion for the defence we had made'. (Holme, *Silver Wreath*, Hook Account, p.65) The rest of his column then slowly inched its way into the post via the ponts. Captain Hallam Parr recorded the 'startling' scene which greeted the first men of the relief force:

> Hundreds of Zulu lying around the building and parapets in every conceivable attitude and posture. In some places they had fallen in heaps over one another – some with the most ghastly wounds from having been too close to the muzzle of the rifles which killed them; others having been consumed by fire from having fallen into the flames of the hospital, as they were killed or wounded. The 24th men, all blackened, torn and weary, many wounded and bleeding, some dead or dying.
>
> Hallam Parr, *Sketch*, p.243

Trooper Fred Symons also vividly remembered the scenes of carnage: 'around the burned hospital lay in heaps the dead bodies of the Zulus. Under the trees in front of the hospital lay three horses still tied to a trunk of the tree.' (Hattersley, *Annals of Natal*, p.150)

Lieutenant Harford's less disciplined NNC were the last to enter the post. Wild, excited scenes ensued as his African auxiliaries

*The tattered remains of the Union Flag, allegedly flown over Rorke's Drift during the siege. (RRWM)*

suddenly broke ranks and 'for some time it was quite impossible to keep the men in hand'. They were:

all around the surroundings of the Fort in a second, crowding about the Zulu dead who were lying thick everywhere, partly, no doubt, from curiosity but I dare say some may have been looking out to identify friends or relations as many of the Natal Kaffirs are refugees from Zululand.

Harford, *Zulu War Journal*, p.36

## Recovery

As Chelmsford and his staff toured the post, a deeply fatigued Chard and Bromhead, relieved temporarily of their exceedingly onerous responsibilities, were at last able to take some time off. Joining their equally exhausted but exultant men, Chard was:

glad to seize an opportunity to wash my face in a muddy puddle in company with Private Bushe, 24th, whose face was covered in blood from the wound in the nose caused by the bullet which had passed through and killed Private Cole, 24th.

Holme, *Silver Wreath*, Chard Account, p.53

It must have been a touching scene emphasising the deep bonds forged between officers and men after this twelve-hour struggle for survival, as 'with the politeness of a soldier… he lent me his towel, or rather a very dirty half of one, before using it himself, and I was very glad to accept it'. There was an unexpected treat for the two parched officers. In the midst of his wrecked and looted wagon, Chard discovered, to his delight, a forgotten bottle of beer. The contents were eagerly consumed by both officers who 'drank it with mutual congratulations on having come safely out of so much danger'. (Holme, *Silver Wreath*, Chard Account, p.53)

There were other greater surprises. As the relief column marched in, several more survivors, in addition to the hospital

*The defenders of Rorke's Drift B Company, 24th Regiment after the battle. A good many men were absent after being invalided home. Colour Sergeant Bourne is on the extreme left and Lieutenant Bromhead is to the left of the front row. (JY)*

escapees, staggered in after experiencing a similar night of terror. Two experiences stood out. One involved the escape of the servant of Colonel Harness RA, who had been left behind sick at Rorke's Drift when the column had crossed into Zululand. He had been unfortunately isolated outside the barricades at the precise moment when the Zulus made their major rush on the hospital. Harford completed the miraculous story of his escape:

> As he would certainly have been shot down by the fire of our own men had he attempted in the darkness to run in and clamber back again, he quickly bolted under a small handcart that had been accidentally left propped up outside against the back of the hospital wall and which (lucky for him but unfortunate for the garrison), was in such a position as to be completely out of the line of fire. Here he remained throughout the night wrapped up in his blanket with the Zulus swarming all around him – many of

them actually jumping onto the cart to try and get onto the roof of the hospital… but none of them, curiously enough, made any attempt to move the cart, in which case he would have been done for. In the morning, however, when the Zulus had decamped and all firing had ceased, to the great astonishment of the garrison, he walked in safe and sound, after about as terrifying experience as any man could have gone through.

Harford, *Zulu War Journal*, p.41

Another who had survived 'a terrifying experience as any man could have gone through' was Lieutenant Chard's own wagon driver, a Cape (black) man who had been tasked with caring for the mules outside the garrison perimeter at the start of the battle. He had, understandably, 'lost his courage on hearing the first firing around the hill'. Abandoning his mules he had retreated into one of the caves in the Oskarsberg Hill. His personal nightmare then began as:

he saw the Zulus run by him and, to his horror, some of them entered the cave he was in, and lying downed commenced firing at us. The poor wretch was crouching in the darkness, in the far depths of the cave, afraid to speak or move, as our bullets came into the cave, actually [killing] one of the Zulus. He did not know from whom he was in the most danger, friends or foe, and came down in the morning looking more dead than alive.

Holme, *Silver Wreath*, Chard Account, p.53

Chard also gratefully recalled how the mules were 'recovered… quietly grazing by the riverside'. Such joyful moments were, however, matched by far more tragic scenes, as for instance poor Private Beckett was also discovered that morning, only to die a few hours later from the assegai wounds to his stomach.

After these initial exuberant, even chaotic, scenes a new sombreness returned to the men of the garrison and the relief force. In Hook's words, 'there was no time to sit down and mope…'.

(Holme, *Silver Wreath*, Hook Account, p.65) With fears of a renewed Zulu attack, three vital tasks had to be implemented. Ironically, the first priority was to feed the starving men of the relief column, and the irrepressible Commissariat officers, Dunne and Dalton, somehow found time and energy to haul out and open up several biscuit boxes for 'us hungry souls'. Captain Harford recalled 'what a God-send it was as it was over two days and two nights since most of us had a mouthful of food'. He added thankfully:

hunger, however, luckily does not affect one like thirst, and one could have gone on much longer as there was plenty of good water. [with the Zulu retreat there was a ready access to the water of the Buffalo River]

Harford, *Zulu War Journal*, pp.36–7

The second essential task was to strengthen the badly damaged defences, for the general and his staff feared another Zulu attack that very evening. Lieutenant Milne recalled that 'as soon as the Column had had some food they were immediately set to work to improve the defences'. (PRO, ADM, 16486, Milne Report) The parapets were heightened further and continued to the edge of the hospital, the remains of the thatched roof of the store were removed and, significantly and belatedly, all the trees in close vicinity were finally cut down, denying the Zulus cover in any future attack. The firepower of the garrison could now be massively increased with three of the column's four 7-pounders brought inside to strengthen the perimeter, and these were targeted towards the river. The fourth gun was located by the right of the Krantz and in the direction in which the Zulu had come the previous night. While Lord Chelmsford himself, Colonel Russell and a few men rode on to Helpmekaar and 'communicated by letter' the good news of the relief to Sir Bartle Frere, several parties of mounted men were deployed to reconnoitre the area.

The third and perhaps most pressing health priority was the burial of the dead. The hundreds of putrefying corpses clearly presented a major threat of disease to the reinforced garrison, 'as decomposition comes on quickly under the hot African sun'. This 'mopping-up' process, in particular the treatment of the Zulu wounded has become one of the most controversial episodes in the history of the Rorke's Drift action. The men of the relief column continued to be staggered by the scene of the terrible killing ground in and around the Rorke's Drift post. Lieutenant Harford, hungrily munching his biscuit ration and casually wandering about the fort, was struck by the appearance of the corpses, coupled with the feeling of:

> devastation after a hurricane, with the dead bodies thrown in, the only thing that remained whole being a circular miniature fortress constructed of bags of mealies in the centre.
>
> Harford, *Zulu War Journal*, p.37

Examining the few British dead still remaining where they had fallen, Harford was particularly struck by the sight of 'one of them – a youngster in the Natal Mounted Police – a very fine specimen of humanity' (almost certainly Trooper Hunter, killed during the retreat from the hospital). For a weary Lieutenant Smith-Dorrien, returning from Helpmekaar, where he had spent the night after his miraculous escape from Isandlwana, the scene confronting him was one of:

> Sheer devastation, his own wagon some two hundred yards away riddled and looted… dead animals and cattle everywhere.
>
> Smith-Dorrien, *Memories*, p.19

The burying of the Zulu dead lasted up to two days, the first day being a particularly 'stiff day… officers and men working together with picks and shovels'. For Captain Hallam Parr, assigned to supervise the burial parties, it proved to be a most repulsive task: 'It was disagreeable work handling the dead naked bodies, many with awful looking wounds.' He added that, although there were sufficient numbers of the Native Natal Contingent to supply strong working parties, it was the British regulars who had to directly dispose of the corpses, as 'the natives have great repugnance to touch a dead body'.

With no carts or even horses, the dead Zulu had to be hauled by 'reims' (ropes of hide) over the ground or carried in rough stretchers. Hallam Parr recorded the stilted, rough conversations of his soldiers engaged in this unpleasant task:

*The memorial at Rorke's Drift, rightly commemorating the great bravery of the Zulu warriors. (EY)*

*The British cemetery at Rorke's Drift. (EY)*

'Come on, you black devil', I heard a man mutter to a dead Zulu he was hauling over the grass, as the body caught against a stone; 'I'm blamed if you don't give more trouble dead nor alive… it's your turn now, comrade, now we've cleared the rubbish out of your way' said another 24th man to a dead soldier, who was found with two or three Zulus stretched almost upon him. 'I'm main sorry t[o] put you away, mate,' continued he, laying the end of a torn sack gently over the dead man's face, 'but you died well and had a soldier's end'.

Hallam Parr, *Sketch*, pp.261–2

## Retribution: War Crimes?

Few, if any, of the Zulu wounded were spared. Many were finished off with their own assegais, or by bayonets or rifle butts, the latter method designed to conserve ammunition. It was a process which had begun even as the relief column arrived. Lieutenant Milne, noting, 'firing still going on at wounded men trying to escape'. The historian M. Lieven in 'Butchering the Brutes' (*History*, 84, October 1999) has interpreted these acts as a major war crime, condoned within an official policy of 'total war'.

A closer examination of the sources, however, reveals that not only did the British claim to have sound military reasons for these otherwise abhorrent practices, but that 'other parties' probably carried out the bulk of the killing. Private Hook recalled one highly dangerous encounter he had with a wounded Zulu which convinced many of the garrison that taking Zulu prisoners or rescuing Zulu casualties had become an unacceptable policy. As he strolled around the garrison perimeter collecting Zulu weapons, 'my own rifle in my right hand and a bunch of assegais over my left shoulder', he:

came across an unarmed Zulu lying on the ground, apparently dead but bleeding from the leg. Thinking it strange that a dead man should bleed, I hesitated and wondered whether I should go on, as other Zulu might be lurking about. But I resumed my task. Just as I was passing, the supposed dead man, seized the butt of my rifle and tried to drag it away. The bunch of assegais rattled to the earth. The Zulu suddenly released his grasp of the rifle with one hand and, with the other, fiercely endeavoured to drag me down. The fight was short and sharp, but it ended by the Zulu being struck in the chest with the butt and knocked to the ground. The rest was quickly over.

Holme, *Silver Wreath*, Hook Account, p.65

After such perilous incidents, Hook recalled we were 'not allowed to go on with our task except in twos and threes'. Captain Hallam Parr summed up the dilemma and defended the necessity of such harsh measures:

When it is remembered that even to count the dead after an action with the Zulus was a service of considerable danger, on account of the wounded Zulus attacking unawares those engaged in this duty, and, that, in some cases, it was on this account actually forbidden, some idea will [be] formed of the difficulty in extending to the brave but savage enemy precisely the same rules that are observed in civilised warfare.

Hallam Parr, *Sketches*, p.264

There were other exceptional but morally far less justifiable reasons for such cruel behaviour – namely revenge and retribution. Many amongst both the Rorke's Drift garrison and the relief force had been incensed at the news of Zulu atrocities conveyed to them by survivors of the earlier Isandlwana massacre. One Rorke's Drift defender, Sergeant George Smith, 2/24th, became a ready believer in such often exaggerated stories. In a letter home, posted just two days after the battle, he justified the widely felt mood of retribution:

The Zulus took one of the band boys and hung him up by his chin on a hook and cut him up in bits… I cannot tell you one quarter of

119

the horrors that have taken place… we have counted the number
of blacks that were killed and shot by my company, there were
over 800, so that they paid dearly for what they killed of our men.

Emery, *Red Soldier*, pp.139–40 and Holme, *Silver Wreath*,
Smith Account, p.61

Private James Cook, a 2/24th member of the relief column, also
angrily wrote home:

The sight at the camp was horrible. Every white man that was
killed or wounded was ripped up and their bowels torn out…

Emery, *Red Soldier*, p.98.

Several other Rorke's Drift defenders had been clearly traumatised
by witnessing the horrendous deaths of several of their comrades,
notably Private Joseph Williams, disembowelled alive outside
the hospital and Drummer Hayden and Sergeant Maxfield,
practically dismembered alive in their hospital beds. Such sights
almost certainly reinforced their beliefs in the earlier horror stories
emanating from Isandlwana survivors.

The resulting extreme anger also manifested itself in the several
lynchings of captured Zulu civilians which took place during the
days after the battle. Lieutenant Smith-Dorrien had been shocked,
on his return from Helpmekaar, to find his *reim* gallows, designed
for drying buffalo hides, used as an execution site:

I saw two Zulus hanging on my gallows and was accused by the
Brigade Major Clery… of having given the order.

He was, however, exonerated:

when it was found it was a case of lynch-law performed by
incensed men who were bitter at the loss of their comrades.

Smith-Dorrien, *Memories*, p.19

Although these acts were even less excusable than the killing of the wounded, there was an understandable element in the actions of often incensed British soldiers for whom the Zulu enemy, in Hallam Parr's words, 'appeared to us to be possessed of savagery beyond description' and who 'fought to kill and undoubtedly killed the wounded and mutilated the bodies'. Moreover, it was clear from this account that some senior British officers at least were opposed to such practices and were trying to restore order to the situation.

There was also considerable evidence to suggest that only a minority of British soldiers were involved in these practices, and that many Zulu wounded died at the hands of Britain's African allies serving in the Natal Native Contingent. Captain Hallam Parr reported that although:

Strict orders were given on the subject but it was impossible to prevent the Natal Natives who were slipping away to their homes, killing, according to their custom, any wounded they came across on their way.

Hallam Parr, *Sketch*, p.263

His view was supported by the NNC Commandant, Hamilton-Browne, who recalled his personal experiences during the immediate aftermath of the Rorke's Drift battle:

During the afternoon it was discovered that a large number of wounded and worn-out Zulus had taken refuge or hidden in the mealie fields near the laager. My two companies of Zulus with some of my non-coms, and a *few* of the 24th, quickly drew these fields and killed them with bayonet, butt and assegai. It was beastly but there was nothing else to do. War is war and savage war is the worst of the lot.

Hamilton-Browne, *Lost Legionary*, p.152

Above all, it is clear that these incidents were not part of a total war or genocidal policy against the Zulu. In his 1878 Regulations for Field Forces, the Commander-in-Chief Lord Chelmsford had laid out strict orders that:

> Natives will be treated with kindness. Commanding Officers will exert their influence with all ranks to prevent their being in any way molestation or oppression.
>
> War Office, Regulations Field Forces South Africa

Strict penalties were laid down for British troops and their African allies. Moreover, in retrospect, the actions of often emotionally charged soldiers at Rorke's Drift, fighting a savage enemy who quite obviously would give not quarter, differs little from, for instance, American and British treatment of their fanatical Japanese enemy during the Second World War at a time in which a much higher level of morality might have been expected.

Whatever the arguments advanced to explain these tragic situations, the consequence was that probably up to 600 Zulu died during or immediately after the Rorke's Drift action. To Lieutenant Chard's official figure of 351 Zulu dead must be added many more who died during the mopping-up operations, or who suffered a lingering death in remote caves, dongas and fields. Sergeant Smith's own estimate of 800 may, in fact, be a more realistic assessment of Zulu losses. Overall, the Zulu probably suffered a 12–15 per cent mortality rate, proportionately comparable to official British losses consisting of seventeen dead (fifteen in action with two, Private W. Beckett and Lance Sergeant T. Williams, dying later of their terrible wounds) amounting to around 10 per cent fatalities.

For many of the brave survivors of Rorke's Drift, the ordeal was not yet over. The often horrific battle wounds took weeks to heal. Thus, Corporal William Allen wrote from Helpmekaar, where many of the wounded were transferred:

> I am getting the better of my wound, more rapidly than could be expected. We got here (that is the sick and wounded) on

the 26th of January and have been waiting [for] an ambulance to convey us down the country, which is expected every day. My arm is mending quickly, though I am sorry I cannot say the same for the other wounded men, who appear to be making no progress towards recovery. I feel thankful to God for leaving me in the land of the living.

Emery, *Red Soldier*, p.141

In the extremely overcrowded, heavily reinforced and cramped conditions of Rorke's Drift and Helpmekaar, it was not long before the 'fourth horseman of the Apocalypse' – pestilence – duly arrived. Thus Captain Walter Parke Jones wrote home in February 1879 disconsolately:

We are still waiting at this beastly unhealthy place until reinforcements come from England. One of my men died from diarrhoea yesterday, and that and fever have knocked nearly all my men over. Quite half of the company is in hospital, really ill, it is most depressing… of course, being crowded together in a fort with rotten meal and other stores, and difficulties about sanitary arrangements, has something to do with the question.

Emery, *Red Soldier*, p.141

An early casualty was the indomitable Lieutenant Chard himself who nearly died from fever and was transferred by ambulance to Ladysmith.

A few miles away at Rorke's Drift, where the original battered defences had now been transformed by the Royal Engineers by the construction of a formidable 8ft stone wall, conditions were equally bad and possibly exacerbated by inadequately buried Zulu dead or the still undiscovered corpses outside the perimeter. In March 1879, Lance Corporal Adams, 2/24th, wrote home from Fort Melvill (the renamed Rorke's Drift building) on 6 March:

We have not received any pay this year yet – we have about forty men in the hospital, sixty more attending the hospital, all sick of dysentery and fever, resulting from un-healthiness because of so many dead being buried around… we generally have about two men die every week.

Emery, *Red Soldier*, p.143–44

Lieutenant Harford blamed a combination of the atrocious wet weather and poor administration:

This terrible state of things, living in such slush, caused a lot of sickness from fever and dysentery which carried off a large number of men and one or two of the officers. Notwithstanding this and the knowledge that the fort was over-crowded, Colonel Glyn declined to have any tents pitched outside to relieve matters, being afraid that the Zulus might sweep down on the place again… no one but the officers and NCOs of the Contingent were allowed outside the fort.

Harford, Zulu War Journal, p.39

In such dark days there were still a few moments of joy. The morale of B Company was undoubtedly uplifted by gifts and money donated by many grateful Natal citizens. Sergeant Smith wrote to his wife in February 1879:

The people of Pietermaritzberg are so well pleased at the manner in which my company kept the stores from being taken by the enemy that they think they cannot do enough for us. They have subscribed £150 for us to buy the troops a lot of clothing, and pens, ink and paper, matches, pipes and a lot of everything, and sent them to us to be given to the troops at Rorke's Drift. They also sent word that they consider we have been the means of saving the whole of the colony from being taken by the Zulus, and I don't think they were far wrong, for if we had left the place and let the enemy take it, nothing would have saved the other parts of the colony from the Zulus' raid.

Emery, *Red Soldier*, p.140

There were other small fillips to morale which became a foretaste of what was to follow. In the quagmire and filth which dominated the fort for two months after the siege, and in which men possessed no more than 'a blanket and the clothes that he stood up in', a special:

exception was made… with 13 Company, 2nd Battalion 24th Regiment, who had made such a gallant defence, and they were housed in the attic of Rorke's Drift house with a tarpaulin thrown over the rafters (from which the thatch had been removed) to shelter them from the wet, a well-deserved honour.

Harford, *Zulu War Journal*, p.38

This did not prevent both Harford and Surgeon Reynolds being 'literally washed out of our sleeping place' on 'one particular night'. A retreat to the eaves of B Company's roof failed to save them, as 'Presently swish came about half a ton of water clean on top of us – B Company were emptying their tarpaulin!!' One wonders if this was a pre-meditated prank by B Company directed against their officers! (Ibid., p.39)

An equally amusing incident, an excellent example of 'Tommy' humour in adversity, helped relieve the post-siege misery. Private Hook became the subject of a long-running hilarious episode. Taken on as a servant by Major Wilsone-Black, whose shrill voice with its Scotch accent could be heard above the fort calling for 'H-o-o-k!', as:

many times a day… the men had their little joke. Whenever Hook was called for they themselves shouted for Hook and then yelled out, 'I think he's hooked it, sir!', which always caused great merriment.

Harford, *Zulu War Journal*, p.41

*Seven VC holders from the 24th Regiment in Brecon for the unveiling of the Zulu war memorial plaque in 1898. Left to right back row: Ex-Pte R. Jones VC, Sgt H. Hook, Ex-Pte W. Jones VC. Front row, sitting: Ex-Pte D. Bell, Col E.S. Brown VC, Ex-Pte F. Hitch VC and L/Cpl J. Williams VC. (RRWM)*

Major Wilsone-Black was soon to be entrusted with a much more sombre task, as Rorke's Drift became a main base for the recovery and burial of the Isandlwana dead. On 4 February he led a small patrol which discovered the assegaied, but still well-preserved bodies of Lieutenants Melvill and Coghill who had tried and failed to save the Colours at Isandlwana, while Harford himself recovered the Queen's Colour case and next day, nearby, in a quiet pool, the tattered remains of the silk Colour itself.

A second, larger patrol visited the battlefield of Isandlwana itself on 14 March, 'a horrid scene of desolation' as the 'still-tainted air' filled their nostrils. Most of the Zulu dead had long been removed by their victorious compatriots, but over 100 wagons were left intact, the bodies of the 24th lying in:

all conditions of horrible decay. Some were perfect skeletons, others that had not been stripped, or only partially so, were quite unapproachable and the stench was sickening; but with few exceptions it was impossible to recognise anyone and the only officer that was seen was discovered by his clothes. Of the regular soldiers the largest found in one place was sixty-eight.

Norris-Newman, *In Zululand with the British*, p.123

For the Rorke's Drift survivors, at least rewards were soon forthcoming. An unprecedented eleven VCs were awarded to: Lieutenants Chard and Bromhead, Acting Assistant Commissary Dalton, Corporal Allen, Privates Hook, Hitch, John Williams, William and Robert Jones, Surgeon Reynolds and Corporal Scheiss. Five men received the Silver Medal for Distinguished Conduct: Colour Sergeant Bourne, 2/24th, Second Corporal Attwood, Army Service Corps, Private Roy, 1/24th, Second Corporal McMahon of the Army Hospital Corps and Wheeler John Cantwell of N/3 Battery, 5th Brigade Royal Artillery.

# THE LEGACY

The Battle of Rorke's Drift fully deserves its elevated status in the annals of British military history, if only as one of the most heroically fought and efficiently conducted small-scale military actions of the last 100-odd years. The British were, from the outset vastly outnumbered by up to thirty to one by their Zulu protagonists. In the context of the relatively confined space of the garrison, and the considerable opportunities for enemy concealment in the shrubs, bushes and caves outside and overlooking the garrison, British technical superiority had been much more limited than some observers have suggested. After the initial, albeit destructive volleys fired against the first wave of Zulu attackers, much (if not the majority) of the fighting was at close quarters. The survival of the garrison depended at its most critical times as much on rifle butts and bayonets as it did on the efficacy of the Martini-Henry Box .45 cartridge. The successful withdrawal from the hospital, for instance, was conducted largely at bayonet and assegai point. Indeed, the incredible closeness and intensity of the fighting was graphically testified to by Lieutenant Chard himself during his post-war extended audience with Queen Victoria in October 1879: 'the fight was at such close quarters that the Zulus actually *took* the bayonets out of the rifles.' (RA QVJ, 12 Oct. 1879)

# Battle Analysis: A Military Assessment

It is now possible to evaluate command and control, and the overall conduct of the battle, more precisely in terms of both modern British military doctrine and the views of contemporary experts, notably Major William Penn Symons. A broad comparison of the events of the Rorke's Drift battle with current key principles of war, namely selection and maintenance of aim; maintenance of morale; offensive action; surprise and concentration of force; economy of effort and security; flexibility; cooperation; and overall sustainability, is instructive.

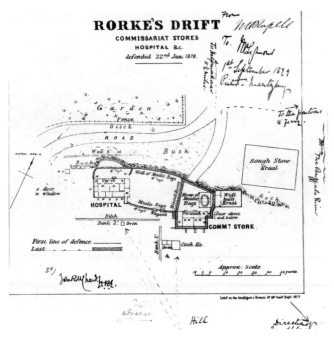

*Lieutenant Chard's famous drawing of the Rorke's Drift battle, showing the main thrusts of the Zulu attack. (RRWM)*

## Selection and Maintenance of Aim

In terms of selection and maintenance of aim, after the initial debate of whether to evacuate the garrison to Helpmekaar, Chard, Bromhead and Dalton collectively clearly defined and selected their defensive aims with commendable speed, only minutes after hearing the news of the Isandlwana disaster and the approach of the Zulu Undi Corps. In such a short time, the arrangement of the defences was a masterpiece with full use made of artificial and natural features. The stone and mud walls of the kraal, hospital and storehouse were fully utilised with a formidable mealie bag barricade along the perimeter, and the front perimeter was also given excellent elevation by its construction along the 3–4ft rocky ledge. These defensive aims were thus attainable and precisely

*Close-up view of the front of the storehouse, clearly revealing the formidable loop-holed walls added after the battle. The final mealie bag redoubt would have been positioned in the immediate foreground. (JY)*

prepared with a number of subsidiary aims, notably a secondary line of defence or fall-back position constructed of biscuit boxes. The broad strategic aim was, moreover, sustained throughout the battle, its defensive principles widely disseminated throughout the garrison, and made the main focus of activity for all the able-bodied men who were fully briefed on their tasks at their designated posts along the barricades.

## Maintenance of Morale

The principle of maintaining morale was also clearly fulfilled, bearing in mind the terrible and unique battle conditions, in which so few British soldiers faced a ferocious enemy who had not only just annihilated a force twelve times their size, but also who patently gave no quarter. In terms of morale, Acting Assistant Commissary Dalton, by his experience, exceptional energy and raw courage, proved to be perhaps the most inspiring figure for the rest of the garrison. Thus Hook admiringly wrote: 'He had formally been a Sergeant-Major in a Line Regiment and was one of the bravest men who ever lived', a man who was seen at the start of the battle literally taunting the Zulus and beckoning them to come on. (Holme, *Silver Wreath*, Hook Account, p.63)

Bromhead's clear popularity and extremely close rapport with his own B Company soldiers also played a key role in the resilience and survivability of the garrison – he constantly patrolled the perimeter, reinforcing weak points and always giving stirring encouragement to his men. For instance, Bromhead had given sympathy and even loaned his revolver to the seriously wounded Private Hitch, their bond of comradeship continuing well after the battle, as Bromhead 'brought his Lordship to see me and was my principal visitor and nurse while I was at the Drift'. (Holme, *Silver Wreath*, Hitch Account, p.62)

Lieutenant Chard also attracted universal admiration from officers and men for his coolness under fire and the competence of his defensive preparations. Of the officers, Dalton, however, clearly occupied a special place in the hearts of the men of B Company. Major General Molyneux, thus recorded a moving incident which occurred at the end of the war:

> After the war, the company of the 24th that had defended Rorke's Drift was marching into Maritzburg amidst a perfect ovation. Among those cheering them was Mr Dalton, who, as a conductor, had been severely wounded there; 'Why, there's Mr Dalton cheering us! We ought to be cheering him; he was the best man there' said the men, who forthwith fetched him out of the crowd and made him march with them. No-one knew better the value of this spontaneous act than that old soldier. The men are not supposed to know anything strategy, and not much about tactics, except fire low, fire slow, and obey orders; but they do know when a man has got his heart in the right place, and, if they had a chance they will show him that they know it. Mr Dalton must have felt a proud man that day.
>
> Molyneaux, *Campaigning in South Africa*, pp.206–7

The outstanding performance of the officers instilled a high degree of determination, confidence and defensive spirit, evident throughout the battle.

## Offensive Action

In terms of the principle of offensive action, both Chard and Bromhead managed the battle exceptionally well and instinctively understood that 'a sustained defence, unless followed by offensive action will only avert defeat temporarily'. Thus Bromhead organised mobile bayonet parties, a crude human form of 'mobile weapons platforms', which were constantly deployed to repel Zulu breakthroughs and thereby effectively depriving them of initiative. 'Fire mobility' was thus fully sustained throughout the siege.

## Surprise and Concentration of Force

Surprise was also a principle which was well exploited by all the officers commanding the garrison of Rorke's Drift. The frequent change of tactics, from sustained volley fire at the start of the siege and the potent use of enfilading fire from the storehouse throughout the siege, followed by the sudden retreat from the hospital perimeter to the well-prepared biscuit box barricades, continually wrong-footed the attacking Zulu force. Allied to this tactic was the extensive use of 'concentration of force' at decisive times and places which accompanied these deceptions. Hence Chard's and Bromhead's constant switching of their soldiers from the front and rear barricades in the first two hours of the siege confused and distracted the Zulu attackers in their constant search for weak points along the perimeter.

## Economy of Effort and Security

Economy of effort – the efficient, at times frugal, use of resources – was also applied extremely well. Lieutenant Bromhead was the pivotal man in terms of the distribution of the ammunition supply. Constantly urging his men of the need to conserve rounds during the later stages of the siege, both he and Chard kept meticulous accounts of the allocation and quantity of ammunition. In this way 'overall security' was achieved, with Chard always guarding an adequate reserve. The judicious allocation of troops and resources was therefore at a premium in the Rorke's Drift siege. In summary, in regard to the three interrelated principles of concentration of force, economy of effort and security, Lieutenants Chard, Bromhead and Acting Assistant Commissary Officer Dalton achieved a high level of excellence.

## Flexibility

Flexibility was also ably demonstrated by the commander, Lieutenant Chard. Without undermining his overall defensive aim, Chard brilliantly modified his plan to rescue the much more dangerous and precarious situation occurring after the retreat from the hospital. In this new tactic, part of the garrison's effort was redeployed, using the lulls in the fight after midnight to construct a last bastion of defence – the mealie bag redoubt. This manoeuvre demonstrated both elasticity of mind and resourcefulness at this critical last stage of the battle. It was a simple, but highly effective solution, designed to both protect the wounded and provide a final elevated concentration of fire for up to forty soldiers.

## Cooperation

Cooperation or teamwork was also ably demonstrated by all members of the garrison. All four 'services' or units present at the siege, the Commissariat, the Army regulars, the Chaplain and even the Army Hospital Corps, each massively supported each other and adapted to each other's requirements; key 'players' such as Byrne, Reynolds, Dalton, Dunne, Chaplain Smith, Bromhead and Chard all worked closely together to carry out essential duties ranging from close-quarter fighting at the barricades to the distribution of food and ammunition. Surgeon Reynolds was, perhaps, the most outstanding example, both attending to the wounded and supplying the hospital under fire with much-needed ammunition. His VC citation highlighted this achievement.

## Overall Sustainability

Overall sustainability was definitely achieved. Chard and Bromhead kept an exceptionally fine balance between 'teeth and tail', wholly maintaining both the physical and psychological condition of the soldiers in order to maintain morale. It was an important achievement, bearing in mind the inexperience and youth of a good many of the garrisons' 2/24th regulars.

## Defining Heroes

Major Penn Symons' contemporary (1890) battle analysis prepared for the Commander-in-Chief the Duke of Cambridge, while giving full credit to the role of the officers at Rorke's Drift, reserved its highest praise for the NCOs and men and, in particular, the heroic deeds of half a dozen private soldiers. He stressed:

> It must be understood that it was essentially a soldiers' fight. Given all credit to the officers who used the best judgement under the circumstances and exhibited prompt action and readiness of resources, given also the confidence with which Lieutenants Chard and Bromhead, young officers both inspired their men, we repeat that it was a fight at long odds of one white man to thirty black savages frenzied with success and slaughter – each individual soldier stood to his post, did his work and duty grandly.
>
> RRWM, Penn Symons Memo to Duke of Cambridge, 21 Feb. 1890

Aside from the commissioned officers, Penn Symons selected seven men whose heroic exploits had played an exceptional role in saving the garrison.

In the hospital fight, four men had been outstanding. Privates Hook and John Williams had fought from room to room, Private Hook being 'last man to leave the hospital'. Privates William and Robert Jones also excelled far beyond the call of duty and had 'defended their post to the last', with 'six out of seven of their patients being saved'. In short, it was 'owing to the personal pluck and exertion of these four men that the last of the patients escaped'.

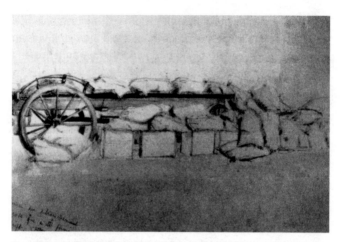

*Henry Degacher's sketch of one of the wagons built into the back wall at Rorke's Drift. (NG)*

Penn Symons also singled out both Acting Commissary Officer Dalton 'badly wounded in the shoulder' and the impressive Corporal Scheiss, who 'deserved the highest praise for their cheery encouragement of the soldiers and the good work they performed in defence'. He again recalled how Dalton 'who had charge of the wagon barricade stood up on one of the wagons and jeered and at the Zulus, daring them to come on and that when... he had no more ammunition left he threw his helmet at some of them crouched behind the covers...' Corporal Scheiss had 'fought like a little tiger – he could not restrain himself but more than once dashed over the barricade, bayoneting a Zulu and got back again'. Two other men, Corporal William Allen and Private Hitch, Penn Symons asserted:

> must also be mentioned for their courageous work and initiative. It was chiefly due to these two men that contact with the hospital was kept up at all. Holding, at all cost, a most dangerous part at the north-east corner of the hospital raked in reverse by the enemy fire from the hill, they were both severely

wounded, but their determined conduct enabled the patients
to be withdrawn from the hospital. When incapacitated from
their firing themselves they continued, as soon as their wounds
had been dressed, to serve out ammunition for their comrades
during the fight.

Overall, it had been 'a gallant defence'. The young soldiers 'backed
each other up and fought splendidly'. They 'never wavered for an
instant' and, despite:

Only a few months of training and influence of esprit de corps,
had become the best and pluckiest 'Warwickshire Lads' and
gloriously upheld the traditions of the old 24th.

## Motivation

Aside from their own survival instincts and loyalty to their officers,
loyalty to 'mates' or comrades constituted a prime motivator for
both the NCOs and rank and file. This had been demonstrated
repeatedly during the hospital fight, as men fought to rescue their
wounded colleagues and was displayed constantly outside on the
barricades as men fought shoulder to shoulder, and also on one
famous occasion, led by Private Hook, formed a bayonet party and
risked their lives to fetch water for their exhausted and wounded
comrades. Such was the intensity of comradeship and 'battlefield
bonding' that some men had even sworn to die in mutual suicide
pacts rather than surrender to such a merciless enemy (notably
Gunner Howard and his comrades in the storehouse at the start
of the attack, and Privates Hitch and Deacon stationed on the
barricades). Regimental pride was also an important motivating
factor for some, especially for the NCOs. Thus, Corporal Lyons
recalled how, 'we were all determined to sell our lives like soldiers
and to keep up the credit of our Regiment'. (Holme, *Silver Wreath*,
Lyons Account, p.61) Colour Sergeant Bourne exuded regimental
pride in his account of the battle:

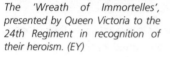

The 'Wreath of Immortelles', presented by Queen Victoria to the 24th Regiment in recognition of their heroism. (EY)

Colour Sergeant Frank Bourne, one of the lynchpins of the Rorke's Drift defence. (RRWM)

Now just one word for the men who fought that night; I was moving about amongst them all the time, and not for one moment did they flinch, their courage and their bravery cannot be expressed in words; for me they were an example all my soldiering days.

Holme, *Silver Wreath*, Bourne Account, p.60

After the debâclé at Isandlwana, recovering regimental honour was clearly at a premium in many men's minds. All men, including the NCOs such as Colour Sergeant Bourne, later took enormous pride in royal honours bestowed on the regiment, notably Queen Victoria's award of the 'Wreath of Immortelles' now preserved in the regimental chapel at Brecon Cathedral. Closely associated with regimental pride was the much less attractive but perhaps understandable motive of seeking revenge for their dead comrades at Isandlwana. Sergeant Smith noted how the Zulu 'paid dearly for what they killed of our men'. (Holme, *Silver Wreath*, Smith Account, p.61)

Religion played a role at this time of great adversity, hence the frequent references to gratitude to God for saving their lives in many of the battle accounts.

While all the individuals mentioned earlier received the Victoria Cross, there were clearly many other unsung heroes amongst the garrison. Lieutenant Chard himself singled out 'Corporal Lyons, Private McMahon, Army Hospital Corps, Privates Roy, Deacon, Bushe, Cole, Jobbins of the 24th and many others'. (See Holme, *Silver Wreath*, Chard Report, p.51 for his several tributes to his men.)

In any assessment of the military significance of Rorke's Drift, a key question is the degree of threat presented by the Zulu enemy to the garrison and to the wider region. At least one recent distinguished writer has played down the status of the assaulting Zulu force to a mere 'raiding party' with the very limited aims of attacking a few border farms in Natal. Thus Professor Laband writes:

> In reality the defence of Rorke's Drift merely diverted a large Zulu raiding party from going about its short term business of ravaging the Buffalo River valley in the vicinity, and not marching on Pietermaritzburg.
>
> Laband, *Kingdom and Colony*, p.115

In fact, the 'raiding party' was a full Zulu corps (the Undi Corps), up to one-fifth of the main Zulu army engaged earlier at Isandlwana. It was a force amounting to approximately 4,000 men, four times or more than one would expect to comprise even an over-large Zulu raiding party. It included the crack uThulwana Regiment, reportedly the king's favourite regiment. Moreover, the Zulu demonstrated exceptional courage and resilience by sustaining a prolonged attack, which included up to at least six major assaults sustained over a period of nearly eight hours (far longer than their compatriots at Isandlwana and at proportionately comparable human cost, with casualties of between 10–15 per cent). No 'raiding party' would even have contemplated such a major and sustained attack, particularly after the heavy losses resulting from the initial British volleys. By their very nature, raiding parties engage in only light 'hit and run' tactics over a wide area and do not tolerate large casualties.

Professor Laband has also suggested that the Undi Corps was an already fatigued force, however there is plenty of contrary evidence to show that it was 'battle ready'. As the Zulu reserve at Isandlwana, the Undi Corps had spent most of the morning of 22 January as virtual spectators of the battle, as their comrades annihilated the British garrison. They had time to eat and rest, probably, as in Zulu tradition, with their backs to the fight. At the most they had been engaged at the tail end of the battle in a few light mopping-up operations, killing isolated fugitives on their slow journey to attack the mission station at Rorke's Drift. As one key Zulu eyewitness recalled:

> The Mbzankomo [uThulwana] regiment merely remained at the Ingwebini river. They danced and just ate merrily. Presently they said 'Oh! Lets go and have a fight at Jim's [the Zulu name for Rorke's Drift]'.
>
> Webb, *A Zulu boy's recollections, Natalia,* December 1978

As the distinguished Zulu War historian Webb further confirms, 'the main body of the Undi lagged behind the other Zulu regiments when the battle began. During the course of the fighting they circled round Isandlwana and moved on to Rorke's Drift.'

Moreover, the 10-mile route to Rorke's Drift from Isandlwana Camp had been conducted at a leisurely pace for a Zulu regiment with, so we have seen, frequent manoeuvrings and stops for traditional snuff taking and to burn isolated farms. Thus the historian Moodie records in *Moodie's Zulu War* their slow progress, the three companies of the Undi Corps advancing in open order from Isandlwana, 'going through various exercises... remaining a long time on the river... and sitting down to take snuff'.

In short, the Zulu regiments who so ferociously attacked Rorke's Drift were an extremely confident, fit unit, anxious to engage in a prolonged battle with the garrison and desperate to gain the full battle honours of their comrades at Isandlwana. In Dabulamanzi's oft-quoted words, he 'wanted to wash the spears of his boys'.

The Zulu longer term objectives were, it can also be argued, potentially very serious, extending far beyond those of a raiding party and were aimed, if some sources are to be believed, at overrunning large parts of the Natal colony. Although Cetshwayo had initially ruled against extending beyond the Natal border, there is strong evidence that the Sihayo fight had already led to a major review of his strategy. Moreover, the Undi Corps' commander, Dabulamanzi – a notoriously individualistic and reckless leader – later revealed his own wider strategic objectives had Rorke's Drift fallen. When Lieutenant Stafford visited his kraal a few years after the war, he significantly asked Dabulamanzi:

> If it had been his intention to invade Natal. He answered that, while initially Cetshwayo had told him that the 'flooded rivers were a bigger king than he was…, had Rorke's Drift fallen I should have taken my army into Natal.
>
> NAM, Stafford Papers

From both the garrison and from contemporary local perspectives, the successful defence of Rorke's Drift had been crucial to saving Natal and the rest of the column. Chaplain Smith, for instance, wrote:

> It was certainly of the utmost strategic importance that this place should not be taken… the safety of the remainder of the Column and this part of the Colony depended on it.
>
> Lummis, *Smith Diary*, p.55

The *Times of Natal* echoed his words: 'Had we lost our position here, I believe the wave of destruction would have gone on into the Colony.' (Lock and Quantrill, *Red Book*, p.102) When, in 1882, the traveller Bertram Mitford asked Mehlokazulu, a 'sub-chief of the iNgobamakhosi Regiment' and a veteran of Isandlwana, what he had perceived to be Natal's strategic position during the war he replied:

not much… how easy it would have been for an impi to 'eat up' the place and kill everyone in it. They would begin at Mkunkundhlovwane (Grey Town) in the morning and finish with Mkukundhlovu (Maritzburg) in the evening.

Mitford, *Through the Zulu Country*, p.81

Penn Symons also reaffirmed the strategic importance of the Rorke's Drift victory:

It was of the utmost importance that Rorkes Drift should not have been captured by the enemy. Had it fallen Helpmekaar would probably have gone also and not only would a great panic have fallen in the Colony of Natal, probably followed by invasion by a triumphant enemy, but the safety of the remainder of Colonel Glyn's Column would have been imperilled.

RRWM, Penn Symons Memo

As a contemporary memorandum by General Grenfell (later Field Marshal Lord Grenfell) revealed, Natal had been extremely vulnerable to attack in the aftermath of the Isandlwana disaster, 'we are working day and night at the defence of Natal. There is nothing to prevent an invasion.'

For the Zulu flushed with the success of Isandlwana, the failure at Rorke's Drift (albeit a heroic failure) was a brutal reminder of the futility of open order attack on a fortified position. One report from a Zulu witness printed in the *Natal Colonist and Mercury* even claimed that some of the Rorke's Drift Zulu commanders had been put to death for 'attacking in the open'. (Lock and Quantrill, *Red Book*, p.102)

Dabulamanzi certainly had made some serious tactical errors and his generalship was, overall, poor. Weaknesses in the Rorke's Drift perimeter had not been exploited. Colour Sergeant Bourne, for instance, was mystified by the Zulu failure to literally pierce the mealie bag wall and thereby collapse it, while several eyewitnesses were amazed at the general Zulu reluctance to use their 'throwing' spears. (Holme, *Silver Wreath*, Bourne Account, p.60) Harford was also astonished to see how the Zulu commanders had failed to set fire to a haystack near the storehouse, which could have severely compromised the garrison's defences. (Harford, p.41) The resultant losses were proportionately comparable to Isandlwana – 2,000–3,000 dead out of a 25,000 attacking Zulu force, and 400–600 out of a 4,000 attacking force at Rorke's Drift. One 'crack regiment', the uThulwana, had been almost destroyed. Even more than the British victory at Inyenzane the same day, Rorke's Drift had been an abject lesson for the Zulu. As one leading colonist put it:

> In its unsuccessful attack upon Lieutenant Gonville Bromhead's Garrison of the 2/24th the uTulwana Regiment, Cetshwayo's regiment lost half its best men… the uTulwana is a crack regiment, some four thousand strong and their signal repulse after twelve hours fierce fighting by the small force has… much damaged the rejoicing of the Zulu Nation.
> NAM, Chelmsford Papers, Chamberlain to Father, 7 Feb. 1879

The extent of Zulu humiliation and its implication for Zulu morale and prestige was revealed by a contemporary Zulu eyewitness:

> The Mbazamkamo (Undi) Regiment was finished up at Jim's – shocking cowards they were too. Our people laughed at them, some said, 'you, you're no men! You're just women, seeing that you ran away for no reason at all like the wind. – You marched off. You went to dig little bits with you assegais out of the house of Jim that had never done you any harm'.
> Webb, *A Zulu Boy's Recollections*, *Natalia*, December 1978

After the Rorke's Drift defeat, the:

> Zulus had no desire to go to Maritzburg. They said 'there are strongholds there'. They thought that they should perish and come utterly to an end if they went there.
> Webb, *A Zulu Boy's Recollections*, *Natalia*, December 1978

The combined casualties of Isandlwana and Rorke's Drift had, indeed, been devastating for the Zulu people. Major General Molyneux, who visited several Zulu kraals after the war, found in one large kraal, 'a lot of wounded' – one had lost two brothers at Isandlwana – his regiment was the Ngobamakhosi', while 'the many little mounds outside, covered with stones, told how many poor fellows had crawled home merely to die'. A Dutch trader, Cornelius Vijn, staying at one of Cetshwayo's kraals, recorded the local impact of the news on 25 January of the terrible losses at Isandlwana and Rorke's Drift. As he lay in a hut talking with Ziwedu (Cetshwayo's brother):

> Our attention was drawn to a troop of people, who came back from their gardens crying and wailing. As they approached I recognised them as persons belonging to the kraal at which I was staying. When they came into or close to the kraal they kept on wailing in front of the kraals rolling themselves on the ground and never quietening down; nay, in the night they wailed so as to cut through the heart of anyone. As this wailing went on, night and day for a fortnight; the effect of it was very depressing; I wish I could not hear it... of the Zulus, according to their account, many thousands had been left behind on the field – Dabulamanzi told me they were buried – never more to return to their homes, and still more were wounded.

Vijn, *Cetshwayo's Dutchman*, pp.28–9

## The Political and Social Significance

The Battle of Rorke's Drift had wider political reverberations extending to the highest level of the Victorian establishment. The news of the earlier military catastrophe at Isandlwana on 11 February 1879 had come as a terrible shock to both the government and people of Britain. As Hicks Beach's somewhat ambivalent despatches immediately before the war had indicated, both Sir Bartle Frere and Lord Chelmsford were likely to pay a heavy political price if the war was not conducted cheaply and with minimum casualties. By mid-February 1879, as the full extent of the tragedy became clear, the 'Izamgoma' ('witch finders') of press and parliament had commenced a vitriolic campaign demanding for the recall of both men. It soon became clear that Disraeli's government needed scapegoats. As one Colonial Office official, Edward Fairfield, cryptically observed, 'the war and, above all, the defeat of Isandula have totally changed the case'. (PRO Minute, Fairfield to Branston, 10 March 1879) *The Times* on 12 February 1879 was much more explicit: 'There is, in fact, little room for doubt that if Lord Chelmsford's invasion had been successful, Sir Bartle Frere's conduct would have been condoned.'

Given this major military disaster 'somebody must be fixed for the blame' as one speaker in the House of Commons so aptly put it. The Prime Minister, the Earl of Beaconsfield Benjamin Disraeli, was particularly stunned by the disaster and, forced to despatch urgent and costly reinforcements, was privately furious with both Frere and Chelmsford. The disaster at Isandlwana would 'change everything, reduce our continental influence and embarrass our resources'. (RA QVJ, Disraeli to HM, 12 Feb. 1879)

In the Commons 'South African debate' for instance, a leading MP, Sir Robert Peel, 'made a really virulent attack on Sir Bartle Frere' and then 'took it into his head to make a still more virulent attack on Lord Chelmsford whom he denounced as being worthy of Admiral Byng'. (RA QVJ, Sir Stafford Northcote to HM, 1 April 1879)

These political attacks were paralleled by fierce attacks on Frere and Chelmsford, emanating from within the Victorian military establishment. Before the results of the Isandlwana Court of Inquiry had been convened, the Adjutant General, on behalf of the Duke of Cambridge, the Commmander-in-Chief of the British Army, had already sent to Chelmsford a highly critical memo regarding the Isandlwana disaster for which he demanded immediate answers. Despite the British victory there, Chelmsford was even criticised for his deployment of the Rorke's Drift supply depot. He was asked:

How did it happen that the post at Rorke's Drift, covering as it did the passage into Zululand, was not put into a state of defence previous to your Lordships advance to Isandula Hill.

NAM Chelmsford Papers, Adjutant General to Chelmsford,
6 March 1879

General Sir Garnet Wolseley and officers from his 'school' were even more vitriolic in their public and private criticism of both Frere and Chelmsford, but particularly Chelmsford. Thus, General Wolseley wrote to his wife that Chelmsford 'had violated every principle of war in his plan of campaign, and has, in fact, courted disaster'. In his private diary, he was even scathing in his criticism of the Rorke's Drift garrison. He wrote:

It is monstrous making heroes of those, who shut in the buildings at Roorke's [sic] Drift could not bolt and fought like rats for their lives which they could not otherwise save.

Preston, *Wolseley's South African Journal 1879–80*, pp.256–7

Earlier on 16 July 1879, after presenting Lieutenant Chard with his Victoria Cross, he acidly remarked:

A more uninteresting or more stupid looking fellow I never saw – Bromhead of the 24th Regiment who was the second in command of the post is a very stupid fellow also.

Such scathing comments were, perhaps, to be expected of a man who was later cheated of victory in the Zulu War by Chelmsford, who went on to win the decisive battle which broke Zulu power at Ulundi on 4 July 1879.

Under such a barrage of attacks from both the military and political establishment, both Frere and Chelmsford made maximum use of the Rorke's Drift victory as a means to both defend their policies and to divert or deflect attention away from the disastrous Battle of Isandlwana. In the weeks leading up to the censure debate, Rorke's Drift became a veritable 'politcal football' between the two sides. Thus on 27 January 1879, only five days after the disaster, Chelmsford informed the Secretary of State for War:

> The defeat of the Zulus at this post and the very heavy losses suffered by them have to a great extent neutralised the effect of the disaster at Isandlwana and it no doubt saved Natal from serious invasion… The cool determined courage displayed by the gallant garrison is beyond all praise… the lesson taught by the defence is most valuable.
>
> PRO CO. 48/489, Chelmsford to Sec State War, 27 Jan.1879

In a letter to the Colonial Office, Sir Bartle Frere staunchly echoed Chelmsford's words. Noting that Chelmsford's orders 'were clearly not obeyed on that terrible day at Isandlwana camp', he continued:

> I will not say a word of blame of those who died so nobly but I should ask attention to the defence of that same night of the Rorke's Drift post by a company of Her Majesty's 24th Regiment against an overwhelming force of Zulus. The latter action is most instructive as illustrating what is the real strength as well as what is the weakness of Cetewayo's military organisation.
>
> PRO CO. 48/489, Frere to Colonial Office, 3 Feb. 1879

Frere then proceeded to give a long page blow-by-blow account of the action. In this simmering political row Frere and Chelmsford received massive support from Queen Victoria and the Royal Family in general.

Their defence cut no ice with their political superiors, but with such evidence presented before her in all these letters, the Queen took an increasingly robust posture against demands for the recall of both Sir Bartle Frere and Lord Chelmsford.

Her revenge was sweet. While Disraeli invited Redvers Buller and Sir Evelyn Wood – two other prominent soldiers in the Zulu campaigns – to his private residence, Hughenden, she publicly fetéd Lord Chelmsford on his return. Equally significantly, the Queen went out of her way to honour the returning heroes of Rorke's Drift, actions which were fully publicised across the country and received wide coverage in the press. In August 1879, the Queen accordingly made a journey from Osborne House to Netley Military Hospital with her private secretary, General Ponsonby. Here, a visit was made to the ward of wounded Rorke's Drift hero, young Private Hitch of the 2/24th, who was:

> very severely wounded in the shoulder affecting the use of his right arm which he cannot raise to his head… he behaved most gallantly at Rorke's Drift defending the Hospital and serving out ammunition to the men long after he was wounded till he fell senseless from exhaustion. He is a tall, good looking young man, with a very determined expression, but very modest and bears a high character.
>
> RA QVJ, 12 Aug. 1879

Before leaving, perhaps as a final sop to critics such as Wolseley, she recorded an extremely rare honour for a private soldier: 'Hitch was brought to the door for me to give him the VC which I told him I did as a reward for his great bravery. He could not say a word and I hear afterwards he fainted'. (Ibid.)

An equally distinguished royal accolade was afforded to Lieutenant Chard on his return from South Africa. He was granted several audiences with the Queen over a three-day period in October 1879. There, he was asked to give a meticulous verbal account of the Rorke's Drift action, the Queen using Chard's earlier despatch to record all the details in her journal. Several other members of the Royal Family were present, and the Queen was even duly instructed by Chard on the Zulu use of an assegai which she had been given earlier as a gift.

The Queen's ostentatious celebration of her 'Rorke's Drift heroes' was mirrored across the country, undoubtedly much to the discomfiture of government, severely embarrassed by the earlier Isandlwana defeat, and those parliamentary critics seeking the recall of both Frere and Chelmsford. *Punch* took the lead with a splendid cartoon celebrating the heroic achievements of Lieutenant Chard and Bromhead, and over the next few months the event became a major feature in numerous popular journals, pamphlets and newspapers. Tributes and scores of poems in the 'Penny Dreadfuls' appeared again and again. Such accolades were perhaps representative of a deeper cultural phenomenon – a new awareness, in an age of distant and poor communication, of the impact of the Empire upon indigenous peoples, if only in a somewhat naïve and heroic 'noble savage' tradition. The Victorian public demonstrated a voracious appetite for all things 'Zulu', admiring their enemy for their exploits as much as they admired their compatriots who fought so valiantly at Rorke's Drift. As the historian Frank Emery in *Red Soldier* observes, 'the moguls of show business were not slow to respond'. Travelling theatre re-enacted the battle across the country, including a troupe of 'genuine' Zulu warriors, allegedly veterans of the battles. The show reached

*In this* Punch *cartoon Lieutenants Chard and Bromhead are saluted for their gallant defence at Rorke's Drift, March 1879.*

Brecon, hard-hit by the Isandlwana losses, but both performances nevertheless attracted healthy audiences (prices ranging from two shillings for front seats and sixpence in the promenade), although the *Brecon County Times* more realistically appraised the show as a circus act of 'Burnt Cork Zulus'! When the show reached London, however, the continuing and deep political sensitivities of the government became abundantly clear. In an astonishing move, the Home Secretary attempted to ban the show 'presumably', as Emery succinctly comments:

> because the Disraeli government was still highly sensitive from the confusion into which they had been plunged by the Zulus. No reminder, not even a public entertainment was welcome.
>
> Emery, *Red Soldier*, pp.144–5 and 254–5

For the general military establishment, the response to the Rorke's Drift victory was equally enthusiastic and longer lasting. The bitter carping of Wolseley and his supporters were ignored and the battle remained a central focus for military displays and re-enactments during and far beyond the Victorian period. The Rorke's Drift veterans were always a central feature of regimental celebrations, especially anniversary dinners, until literally the end of their lives. The last public appearance of two of the longest-lived veterans, Colour Sergeant Bourne and Private Jobbins, probably occurred at the 1934 Ravensworth Castle, 'Northern Command Tattoo' where a splendid re-enactment of the battle took place.

The battles' significance was never lost to popular culture, and re-emerged in a spectacular way with the making and release of the acclaimed action film *Zulu* in 1964. The film not only recreated (if often with poetic licence) the events of the battle in Victorian heroic tradition, emphasising coolness and discipline under fire and extreme bravery on the British side, but also reflected the new post-war critical style of film-making, with a strong emphasis upon Zulu culture, gallantry and sacrifice. Both Briton and Zulu are portrayed as, to some extent, tragic victims of a brutal 'imperial war'. In the words of film critic Trevor Willsmer, the film was '*our* epic, a celebration of national courage (but not nationalism with its eyes "wide open")'. Such balanced treatment probably explains the mass appeal of a film which, in 1960s multi-racial Britain:

> reflected the post-war mood of residual pride but one which also carried a new awareness of the harsher realities and consequences of empire-building for both conquerors and conquered.
>
> Yorke, 'Cultural myths and realities', in S. Carruthers and I. Stewart (eds) *War, Culture and the media* (Hicks Book, 1996) and T. Willsmer, *'Zulu'*, *Movie Collector*, 1974

# Conclusion

The political and military significance of the Battle of Rorke's Drift has been significantly underestimated. The victory at this post, achieved by a few British soldiers against massive odds, provided a major deterrent to further Zulu inroads into Natal, at a time when Chelmsford's main column was totally demoralised and Natal's defences severely compromised. Despite claims from some historians that the defenders were over-rewarded and lionised to compensate for, or divert attention from, the earlier Isandlwana defeat, the scale and intensity of the fighting fully justified the award of eleven VCs and must be treated in isolation from the earlier catastrophic defeat at Isandlwana. For these reasons, Rorke's Drift was of far more significance than the other British victory at Inyenzane the same day, and decisively demonstrated the efficacy of fortified positions against Zulu open order attack. Indeed, the battle undoubtedly became a model for the rest of the campaign and subsequent British campaigns against 'native enemies' (notably the Sudan). The treatment of Zulu wounded was morally reprehensible but perhaps understandable in the contemporary context of such a brutalised conflict, in which prisoners were rarely taken by either side.

The battle was significant in other ways. It was a major psychological boost to the Victorian public after the Isandlwana disaster and became an enduring symbol of, initially, British heroism, and ultimately Zulu heroism. Its political significance must not be underestimated. The victory played an important role in the post-Isandlwana debate and was extensively used by both Frere and Chelmsford and their supporters to justify and defend their policies. If both men had, in different ways, exceeded or neglected their duties, their subsequent ambivalent treatment by their political masters, in which the military importance of Rorke's Drift was largely ignored or unrecognised, must also be the subject of severe censure.

# ORDERS OF BATTLE

## British Army

Lieutenant J.R.M. Chard,
5th (Field) Company, Royal
Engineers, commanding

Staff: Sergeant G.W. Mabin

### 'N' Battery, 5th Brigade, Royal Artillery

Bombardier T. Lewis

Wheeler J. Cantwell

Gunners: A. Evans and
A. Howard

### 5th (Field) Company, Royal Engineers

Driver E. Robson

### 1st Battalion, 24th (2nd Warwickshires) Regiment of Foot

Sergeant E. Wilson

Privates: W. Beckett;
P. Desmond; W. Horrigan;
J. Jenkins; E. Nicholas; T. Payton;
W. Roy; H. Turner; J. Waters

### 2nd Battalion, 24th (2nd Warwickshires) Regiment of Foot

Lieutenant G. Bromhead

Colour Sergeant F.E. Bourne

Sergeants: H. Gallagher;
R. Maxfield; G. Smith;
J. Windridge

Lance Sergeants: J. Taylor;
T. Williams

Corporals: W.W. Allan; G. French;
J. Key; (1112) J. Lyons; A. Saxty

Lance Corporals: W. Bessell;
W. Halley

Drummers: P. Galgey; P. Hayes;
J. Keefe; J. Meehan; T. Chester;
J. Chick; T. Connors; W. Cooper;
G. Davies; W.H. Davis; T. Daw;
G. Deacon; M Deane; J. Dick;
W. Dicks; T. Driscoll; J. Dunbar;
G Edwards; J. Fagan; E. Gee;
J. Hagan; J. Harris; G. Hayden;
F. Hitch

Privates: R. Adams; J. Ashton;
T. Barry; W. Bennett; J. Bly;
J. Bromwich; T. Buckley;
T. Burke; J. Bushe; W.H. Camp;
A.H. Hook; J. Jobbins; E. Jones;
R. Jones; W. Jones; P. Judge;
P. Kears; M. Kiley; D. Lloyd;
T. Lockhart; J. Lodge; T.M. Lynch;
(1441) J. Lyons; J. Mauley;
J. Marshall; H. Martin; C. Mason;
M. Minehan; T. Moffatt;
A. Morris; F. Morris; T. Morrison;
J. Murphy; W. Neville;
R. Norris; W. Osborne; S. Parry;
W. Partridge; S. Pitts; T. Robinson;
J. Ruck; E. Savage; J. Scanlon;
A. Sears; G. Shearman;
J. Shergold; J. Smith; T. Stevens;
W. Tasker; F. Taylor; T.E. Taylor;
J. Thomas; P. Tobin; W. J. Todd;
R. Tongue; (1395) J. Williams;
(934) J. Williams (1398)
J. Williams; C. Woods.

## 90th (Perthshire Volunteers) Light Infantry

Corporal J. Graham

## Commissariat and Transport Department

Assistant Commissary
W.A. Dunne

Acting Assistant Commissary
J.L. Dalton

Acting Storekeeper L.A. Byrne

## Army Service Corps

Second Corporal F. Attwood

## Army Medical Department

Surgeon L.H. Reynolds

Mr Pearce (surgeon's servant)

## Army Hospital Corps

Corporal R. Miller

2nd Corporal M. McMahon

Private T. Luddington

Honorary Chaplain, Weenen
Yeomanry

The Revd G. Smith, Vicar of
Escort

## Natal Mounted Police

Troopers: R. Green; S. Hunter;
H. Lugg

## Natal Native Contingent

Lieutenant J. Adendorff

Corporals: M. Doughty;
J.H. Mayer; C. Scammel;
C.F. Schiess; J. Wilson

Native Private (Name Unknown)

Civilian

Mr Daniells (Ferryman)

## British and Colonial Casualties

## Killed in Action

*1st Battalion, 24th (2nd Warwickshires) Regiment of Foot*

Privates: W. Horrigan; J. Jenkins;
E. Nicholas

*2nd Battalion, 24th (2nd Warwickshires) Regiment of Foot*

Sergeant R. Maxfield

Privates: R. Adams; J. Chick;

T. Cole; J. Fagan; G. Hayden;
J. Scanlon; J. Williams

*Commissariat and Transport
Department*

Acting Storekeeper L. A. Byrne

*Natal Mounted Police*

Trooper S. Hunter

*Natal Native Contingent*

Native Private (Name Unknown)

## Wounded in Action

*1st Battalion, 24th (2nd
Warwickshires) Regiment of
Foot*

Private W. Beckett, mortally
wounded. Died of wounds
23 January 1879

Private P. Desmond, slightly
wounded

Private J. Waters, severely
wounded

*2nd Battalion, 24th (2nd
Warwickshires) Regiment of
Foot*

Lance-Sergeant T. Williams,
mortally wounded. Died of
wounds, 25 January 1879

Corporal W.W. Allan, severely
wounded

Corporal J. Lyons, dangerously
wounded

Drummer J. Keefe, slightly
wounded

Private J. Bushe, slightly
wounded

Private F. Hitch, dangerously
wounded

Private A.H. Hook, slightly
wounded

Private R. Jones, slightly
wounded

Private J. Smith, slightly
wounded

Private W. Tasker, slightly
wounded

*Commissariat and Transport
Department*

Acting Assistant Commissary
J.L. Dalton, severely wounded

*Natal Mounted Police*

Trooper R. Green, slightly
wounded

*Natal Native Contingent*

Corporal C. Scammell,
dangerously wounded

Corporal C.F. Schiess, slightly
wounded

## Killed

Corporal W. Anderson (by
British fire)

## Zulu Force

### Undi Corps

### Commander: Prince Dabulamanzi Ka Mpande

iNdluyengwe, 500–700

uThulwana

iNdlondlo

uDloko

(Total 3,000–3,500)

# FURTHER READING

## Recommended Archives

Public Record Office (PRO) (now National Archives), Kew (Colonial (CO) and War Office (WO) files), National Army Museum (NAM), Royal Regiment of Wales Museum (RRWM), Royal Logistical Corps Museum (RLCM), Army Medical Corps Museum (AMCM), Royal Archives Windsor (RA), Killie Campbell Library, South Africa.

## Select Bibliography

Bancroft, J., *Rorke's Drift* (Spellmount, 1988)
—, *Zulu War VCs* (Private print, Bancroft,1992)
Barthorp, M.A., *Pictorial History of the Zulu War* (Blandford Press, 1979)
Baynham Jones, A., and L. Stevenson, *Rorke's Drift By Those Who were There* (Stevenson publishing, 2003).
Bennett, I.H.W., *Eyewitness in Zululand* (Greenhill Books, 1989)
Castle, I., *British Infantryman in South Africa, 1877–81* (Osprey, 2003)
Clarke, S. (ed.), *Invasion of Zululand 1879* (Brenthurst Press, 1979)
David, S., *Zulu: The Heroism and Tragedy of the Zulu War of 1879* (Penguin Books, 2004)
Duminy, A., and C. Ballard (eds), *The Anglo-Zulu War: New Perspectives* (University of Natal Press, 1981)
Emery, F., *Red Soldier, Letters from the Zulu War, 1879* (Hodder and Stoughton, 1977)
Greaves, A., *Rorke's Drift* (Cassell, 2002)
Greaves, A., and I. Knight,*Who's Who in the Zulu War*, 2 vols (Pen and Sword, 2006)
Guy, J., *The Destruction of the Zulu Kingdom* (Longman, 1979)

# Further Reading

Hallam-Parr, Captain H.A., *Sketch of the Zulu and Kafir Wars*, (C. Kegan and Paul, 1880)

Hamilton-Browne, Colonel G., *A Lost Legionary in South Africa* (T. Werner Laurie, *c*.1913)

Harford, H.D., and D. Child (ed.), *The Zulu War Journal of Colonel Henry Harford* (Shuter and Shooter, 1978)

Hattersley, A.F., *Later Annals of Natal* (Longmans, 1938)

Holme, N., *Silver Wreath; Being the 24th Regiment at Isandlwana and Rorke's Drift 1879* (Samson Books, 1979)

Knight, I., *Zulu Rising: The Epic Story of Isandlwana and Rorke's Drift* (Macmillan, 2010)

—, *The Battles of Isandlwana and Rorke's Drift* (Windrow and Greene, 1992)

Laband, J., *Lord Chelmsford's Zululand Campaign, 1878–9* (Army Records Society, 1994)

—, *Rope of Sand, The Rise and Fall of the Zulu Kingdom in the Nineteenth Century* (Jonathan Ball, 1995)

—, *Rorke's Drift 1879: 'Pinned Like Rats in a Hole'* (Osprey, 2003)

Laband, J., and P. Thompson, *Kingdom and Colony at War* (N&S Press, 1990)

Lummis, W.M., *Padre George Smith of Rorke's Drift* (Wensum Books, 1978)

Molyneaux ,W.C.F., *Campaigning in South Africa and Egypt* (Macmillan, 1896)

Moodie, D.C.F., *Moodie's Zulu War* (reprint, N&S Press, 1988)

Morris, D.R., *The Washing of the Spears* (Jonathan Cape, 1966)

—, *Nothing Remains But to Fight; The defence of Rorke's Drift* (Greenhill Books, 1993)

Mitford, B., *Through the Zulu Country: Its Battlefields and its People* (Kegan, Paul, Trench and Co., 1883)

Norris-Newman, C.L., *In Zululand with the British throughout the war of 1879* (W.H. Allen, 1880)

Smith-Dorrien, H., *Memories of Forty Years Service* (John Murray, 1925)

Snook, Lieutenant Colonel M., *Like Wolves on the Fold; The Defence of Rorke's Drift* (Frontline Books, 2010)

Yorke, E.J., *Zulu, The Battle for Rorke's Drift* (The History Press/Tempus, 2005)

Young, J., *They Fell like Stones: Battles and Casualties of the Zulu War* (Greenhill Books, 1991)

# INDEX

# Index

Harness, Colonel  113
Hayden, Private Garrett  90, 120
Helpmekaar  40, 49, 50, 54, 64, 103, 105, 106, 115, 116, 120, 122–123, 130, 142
Hicks Beach, Sir Michael  15–17, 34–36, 144
Hitch VC, Private Frederick  42–44, 57, 66–70, 72, 75, 77–81, 84–85, 92, 100–101, 126–127, 131, 136–137, 148
Hook VC, Private Henry  19, 43, 45, 53–55, 60, 64, 65, 72, 74, 83, 84, 87–93, 95, 98, 100–101, 106, 107–110, 114–115, 118–119, 125–127, 131, 135, 137
Horrigan, William  84, 90
Hospital  19, 44, 45, 49, 51, 55, 57–59, 61–63, 69, 70, 74–76, 78–82, 83–97, 101–105, 109, 111–116, 120, 128, 130, 133–137, 139
Howard, Gunner A.  9, 70, 88, 98, 137
Hunter, Trooper S.  94, 116
*Ikilwa* (Zulu stabbing spear)  69
*Impi* (Zulu army)  27, 40, 41, 63, 66, 109, 142
'*Impondo zankomo*' ('beasts horns' Zulu formation)  31, 33, 40
*Indunas* (Zulu Commanders)  30, 32, 33, 69, 84
Isandlwana  10, 15, 23, 25, 26, 27, 33, 35, 36, 38–42, 46, 47, 50–52, 54, 59, 64, 77, 87–88, 109, 116, 119–120, 126, 130, 138–147, 149–152
*Izijula* (Zulu throwing spear)  69
Jenkins, Private J.  94
Jobbins, Private J.  93, 109, 139, 150
Jones, Captain Walter Parke  123
Jones VC, Private Robert  83–84, 93–94, 126–127, 135
Jones VC, Private William  83–84, 92–94, 126–127, 135
Ka Maphitha, Zibhebhu  40, 42
Knobkerrie (Zulu weapon)  29, 62, 75
Lewis, Bombardier T.  94
Lugg, Trooper Harry  50, 59–60, 71–72, 74, 94, 97–98
Lyons, Corporal J.  67–68, 70–72, 77, 137, 139
Martini-Henry rifle  20–22, 28, 37, 59, 69, 70, 71, 77, 79, 100, 103, 128
Maxfield, Sergeant Robert  70, 93, 120
Mayer, Corporal J.H.  94
McMahon, Second Corporal M.  127, 139
Mealie-bag redoubt  95, 130, 134
Melvill, Lieutenant  126
Milne, Lieutenant Archibald Berkeley  56, 109–110, 115, 118
Molyneux, Major General W.C.F.  132, 144
Natal  9, 12, 13, 15, 23–24, 34, 37, 41–42, 48, 51, 112, 124, 139, 141–143, 147, 151
Natal Mounted Police  23, 50, 60, 94, 116
Natal Native Contingent (NNC)  23–24, 40, 50, 53, 57, 64–65, 94, 111, 116, 121
Native Natal Horse (NNH)  23, 40, 50, 63, 64
oNdini  24, 17, 30, 38,
Orange Free State  11
Oskarsberg (or Shiyane) Hill  51, 62, 68–69, 72–73, 76–77, 96, 110, 114

Pearson, Colonel Charles  26
Pietermaritzburg  124, 139
Pulleine, Lieutenant Colonel Henry  39
Punch magazine  36, 149
Reynolds VC, Surgeon Major James Henry  43, 51, 54, 55, 61–67, 70, 72, 74, 81, 82, 88, 92–96, 99, 107, 109, 125, 127, 134
Roy, Private W.  127, 139
Royal Engineers  46, 47, 87, 123
Russell, Major Cecil  110, 115
Russell, William  20
Savage, Private E.  91
Scammell, Corporal C.  81
Shaka, Chief  11, 30–31, 69
Scheiss VC, Corporal Christian  75, 80, 127, 136
Shepstone, Theophilus  14, 16–17
Sihayo, Chief  25, 27, 37, 45, 89, 94, 141
Silver Medal for Distinguished Conduct  127
Smith, Chaplain George  51, 63, 69–70, 72, 75, 77, 79–82, 84, 89, 94–95, 134, 141
Smith, Sergeant George  50, 96, 119, 122, 124, 138
Smith-Dorrien, Lieutenant General  45–46, 116, 120
South Africa  9–16, 22, 25, 47, 48, 148
Spalding, Major Henry  43, 46–49
Stevenson, Captain (sometimes spelt Stephenson)  24, 48, 57
Storehouse  44, 49, 57, 74, 81, 95, 130, 133, 137, 143
Symons, Major Penn  129, 135–136, 142
Symons, Trooper Fred  111
Transvaal Republic  11–13, 16, 17, 27, 34
Victoria Cross  83, 126, 127, 134, 139, 146, 148, 151
Victoria, Queen  10, 14, 15, 18, 47, 128, 138, 147
Vijn, Corenelius  144
Walsh, Lieutenant  110
Waters, Private John  53, 68, 84, 91–92, 105
Whitton, Colonel  88
Williams, Lance Sergeant T.  56, 122
Williams VC, Private John  83–84, 90–92, 126–127, 135
Williams, Joseph  90, 120
Wilsone-Black, Major  125–126
Windridge, Sergeant  57
Witt, Reverend Otto  51, 59, 63, 91
Wolseley, General Sir Garnet  82, 146, 148, 150
Wood, Sir Evelyn  147
*Wreath of Immortelles*  138
Zulel Rorke's Drift memorial  117
Zulu Army  10, 24, 26, 39, 42
  iNdlondlo Regiment  28
  iNdluyengwe Regiment  28, 50, 70, 74
  uDloko Regiment  28, 41–42
  Undi Corps  28, 40, 41, 47, 78, 130, 139–141, 143
  uThulwana  27, 28, 139, 140, 143,
Zulu rituals  32, 99, 140
Zululand  13, 14, 18, 19, 23, 24, 25, 30, 37, 38, 41, 112, 113, 146

159

# EXPLORE HISTORY'S MAJOR CONFLICTS WITH
## BATTLE STORY